RAISING EYEBROWS

CONFESSIONS OF A BEVERLY HILLS MAKEUP ARTIST

BOBBE JOY

BJD PUBLISHING | BEVERLY HILLS, CA

Published by
BJD Publishing | Beverly Hills, CA
www.bobbejoycosmetics.com

Publisher's Cataloging-in-Publication Data
Bobbe Joy.

    Raising eyebrows : confessions of a Beverly Hills makeup artist / Bobbe Joy. – Beverly Hills, CA : BJD Pub., 2020.

    p. ; cm.

    ISBN13: 978-0-9601027-0-9

    1. Dawson, Bobbe Joy. 2. Makeup artists—California—Beverly Hills—Biography. 3. Beauty culture. I. Title.

    TT955.B63 B63 2020
    646.72092--dc23   2020908634

Project coordination by Jenkins Group, Inc.
www.BookPublishing.com

Front cover author photo by Ian Dawson
Cover design by Yvonne Fetig Roehler
Interior design by Brooke Camfield

Printed in the United States of America
24   23   22   21   20   •   5   4   3   2   1

CONTENTS

FOREWORD

For forty years, Bobbe Joy and I have had an enduring friendship. I thought I knew everything about her. Now that I've read her book, I am astonished to find out things I had no idea about, things that are fascinating and very surprising!

Bobbe is a woman whom other women look at and think, "Why can't I look like her?" She's an exquisite woman, a successful businesswoman, a hardworking, generous person, and a devoted, loving wife, mother, grandmother, and friend. She has great wisdom and a clever, witty sense of humor that makes her so much fun!

One of the greatest things I love about my friend Bobbe is her creativity and brilliant knowledge about makeup. With her enormous talent as a makeup artist, she has made up some of the most famous, interesting people, and she has lived an exciting life that she writes about in this candid memoir.

When you have someone come into your life and they become a true friend, it's a gift. Bobbe Joy is my gift, and her life story is powerful and captivating.

Barbara Mandrell

INTRODUCTION

It's 4:00 in the morning. I can't sleep. I have just spent an entire day looking at photographs that span the entirety of my seventy-five years. From a young insecure girl, I've traveled a long, long way to find my own voice and use it. I have, hopefully, inspired my clients, friends, and sometimes even my family by sharing what took me years to learn.

This has been a catharsis. I've been through analysis (formally) by examining each chapter of my life and, hopefully, channeling that information into positive change that will impact others.

Nothing good comes easy, as they say, and finding my way was sometimes challenging, to say the least. And, although there were times I wanted to pull the covers over my head, I persevered.

That I'm grateful for all I have, and all I have achieved, is an understatement.

My mother instilled in me a responsibility to be a good person, explore everything, and try to be the best at whatever I chose to do. My father taught me my work ethic: show up, work hard, keep learning, and be creative. In fact, they both gave me the creative gene, and I took it and ran with it.

I am proud of my children; I definitely passed on that creative gene, and they ran with it too!

Now I am watching four incredible grandchildren follow in their footsteps. Those genes are strong.

With a love for traveling the world, I have had the opportunity to share my adventures with my incredible clients and friends. I know I've inspired some of them to go to places they might never have seen.

I didn't realize how important community was until forty-two years ago when I moved to Beverly Hills and got involved in working and community service. I love our little five-square-mile city and feel blessed to be a part of so many wonderful friendships.

Here are some of the life lessons I want to share:

- Give back—it empowers you.
- Find your voice—use it to inspire others.
- Share—it will truly make you happy.
- Laugh—it will give you power.
- Love—it will sustain you.

Thank you again for being a part of this life I have been so fortunate to live.

BOBBE

A GOOD LITTLE GIRL

It's not your job to like me, it's mine.

—BYRON KATIE

I was born Roberta Joy Singer on November 6, 1944. The earliest message I got from my parents was "Life is meant to be happy," and I believed them. I was an only child, and they meant the world to me. I did everything I could to please them, but for some unknown reason, by the time I entered grammar school, I had begun to suffer a series of mysterious ailments: stomach cramps, heart palpitations, and a stutter. I could see the concern in my parents' eyes. I was six years old and already feeling as if whatever worries they had were my fault. I longed for a way to make them happy again. And then it struck me: all I had to do was to be the best little girl in the world.

• . •

In the 1950s we were living an idyllic life in Studio City, a bedroom community in the San Fernando Valley of Los Angeles. It was a picture-perfect neighborhood of low ranch-style homes with neatly mowed lawns, white picket fences, and swimming pools. Twenty years earlier San Fernando Valley had been an agricultural landscape of cattle ranches and citrus groves, but in the post–World War II housing boom, the cattle and fruit trees moved out, and the people moved in—thousands of them, filling cookie-cutter tract homes designed for returning GIs, as fast as they could be built. Here and there a reminiscent orange or lemon tree still grew, but now it was sturdy elms and oaks that lined the curbsides, providing the leafy canopy that turned a bland housing development into a welcoming community.

By the time my family moved to the San Fernando Valley from the Los Feliz area near Griffith Park, Studio City was known as a collection of higher-priced homes: Spanish-style haciendas and low-slung ranch houses, built for the well-paid artists and craftsmen employed at the nearby movie studios. My father, Louis "Lou" Singer, was one of those studio artists, a musician whose work could be heard on some of the finest movie scores of the day. He was a percussionist who played drums, vibraphone, marimba, xylophone, tympani, cymbals, and all the exotic bells and shakers that make up the drummer's kit. According to his peers, Lou Singer was one of the finest drummers to come out of the Big Band era. After touring with famed band leaders like Artie Shaw and Woody Herman, he became a first-call percussionist for some of the top film composers, including Henry Mancini, Leonard Bernstein, and Jerry Goldsmith. The 1950s was the heyday of motion picture scoring, and every big movie lot had a dedicated sound stage where great orchestral music was being churned out day and night.

In between movie jobs there were endless recording sessions for all the major record labels: Columbia, RCA Victor, Decca, Capitol, and Mercury. I remember my dad coming home after spending a day working with Frank Sinatra or Rosemary Clooney and hearing him mention their names casually, like they were his close friends. He wasn't bragging or boasting; it was his normal conversation, and it made me realize that famous stars were real people, just like my dad.

In the 1950s my father traveled with Liberace, the flamboyant pianist who was famous for his sequined tuxedos and the ornate candelabra that decorated his grand piano. My parents were fortunate enough to travel to Cuba with Liberace prior to the Castro Revolution and to Las Vegas in 1955, when Liberace opened the Riviera Hotel. When I was old enough, they would take me with them, and I remember the excitement of staying at fancy hotels, walking through the Vegas casinos, attending shows in the lavish nightclubs, and being part of my father's world. One Sunday afternoon Liberace invited us to his amazing house in Sherman Oaks, where the pool was shaped like a piano—keys and all! I met his brother George and his beloved Mama, and even though I was very young, I appreciated the fact that this visit was a big deal. I still have an ice bucket decorated with crystal chandeliers, candelabras, and pianos that Liberace gave my parents as a Christmas gift.

When I was in my teens, my father would sometimes let me come to the recording studio with him and occasionally even bring a friend. We were privileged to sit in the recording booth along with the engineer and the record producer, watching with fascination as they turned dials and adjusted sound levels. I especially loved it when the producer spoke over his booth microphone to my father: "Hey, Lou, can you give me an eerie sound in bar twenty?" My father would reach into his black leather case and pull out some magical instrument he had made in his home workshop—some cylinder, rigged with pieces of brass, which he lightly strummed with his fingers to produce exactly the right ethereal jangle to fit the moment. "Perfect!"

the producer would shout, while all the musicians in the orchestra nodded in approval. I was proud to see my dad in this setting and to know how respected he was by his peers. I thought he was cool, and so did all my friends.

My mom, Ruth Cohen Singer, had artistic talents as well and created beautiful hand-painted china, but in accordance with the social norms of the day, her talents were seen only as a hobby. Her expected role was to be a stay-at-home wife and mother and to appreciate the comfortable life my father provided. They spent time with other musicians and their wives, often dining at lovely restaurants. My mom had a coterie of Valley housewife friends who enjoyed the same things she did—shopping, playing mahjong, and doting on their children—but whose inner lives went mostly unheeded.

My parents could afford to treat me like a little princess, and they did. They introduced me to music, culture, and social graces. I wore white gloves and attended luncheons and fashion shows with my mother at high-class department stores, where I was mesmerized by the beautiful runway models. I would study their stylish moves and practice at home in my mirror, dreaming that one day I would be the model parading before the admiring crowd, bending my arm just so to show an elegant cuff or turning gracefully to reveal a strapless bodice. Even at an early age I adored fashion detail and carefully analyzed what the models wore and how they wore it, what shoes went with what style dress, what scarf with what sweater, and how colors played against each other. I bought fashion magazines and studied how the models styled their hair and did their makeup. I had an extremely analytical mind and became obsessed with everything that had to do with fashion.

My mother admired the svelte bodies of the runway models as much as I did, but her natural figure was a plump Eastern European body. It was obvious that she would never achieve the slender figure she so admired. The more weight she put on, the more I became her surrogate, a little doll she could dress up in fashionable clothes. Shopping became our favorite bonding activity, and for better or worse, I became the main focus of her attention.

To the outside world the Singers were a family straight out of *Father Knows Best,* the popular TV series that celebrated the patriarchal norms of the day. Every evening the dad came home from a hard day's work to be greeted by his loving family: the mom would have a home-cooked meal waiting on the stove, and the adoring children would stand in line eagerly anticipating a hug and a kiss from their loving daddy. That was us. My parents were considered a great couple. They threw barbecues and pool parties, and our mandate as a family was to be normal and happy—and God knows we tried, really hard.

While my dad was enjoying his career as a successful musician, my mother was playing her minor role as housewife and mother with a vengeance, pouring a torrent of thwarted ambitions into the tiny cup of her life. She was a demanding perfectionist, which earned her the nickname of "the sergeant" among our extended family. She barked orders like "Hurry up!

Get it done! Don't argue! Clean your room!" She could launch a barrage of searing verbal abuse that withered the intended target— most often me.

But there was another side to my mother, one that I greatly admired. She was a smart, level-headed woman who had the business sense to handle the family finances and keep us safe from the pitfall that so many musicians, including my father, often face: an inability to deal with money. He was the artist, and she was the practical businesswoman. While Lou was enjoying the spotlight and being praised for his talents, Ruth was building a solid financial future for our family, but her accomplishments went unrecognized and often underappreciated. It was a recipe for disaster.

Anyone who has ever worked in the high-pressure environment of show business knows that the flip side of all the glamour is raging insecurity. Everyone is gunning for your spot, and even the smallest mistake—a wrong note, a missed cue, any sign that you might not be as good as you are thought to be—can do real damage to an already fragile artistic ego. There were times when my father would return home from a recording session in a foul mood and we would tip-toe around him. An overcooked steak or a tasteless dinner was all the excuse he needed to explode with a volcanic rage that had been building up in him all day. My mother, harboring her own resentments, never backed down but would go toe-to-toe with him, and in no time our happy household would become a battleground on which my mother and father bludgeoned each other with hateful words in a violent quarrel that would last well into the night. I would hide behind the Dutch doors of my bedroom curled into a ball, my hands over my ears, my tear-filled eyes shut tight, crying out hopelessly, "Stop it! Stop it!" My inability to stop my parents' vile behavior reinforced my feelings of worthlessness. No matter how hard I tried, I never was good enough to stop them. A deep sense of failure had already taken root in me, and in time it grew increasingly more difficult to rationalize the glamorous public life of my parents with their deeply damaged private life. No wonder I suffered from stomach aches and other chronic illnesses—and that stutter!

LOVE AMONG
THE CHICKENS

Rejoice with your family in the beautiful land of life.

—ALBERT EINSTEIN

Let me tell you a little bit about my grandparents. All four of my grandparents came to the United States from Eastern Europe, either the Ukraine or Poland. They were immigrant Jews who, after years of suffering anti-Semitic persecution, courageously left their families in the early 1900s to come to America.

Both my grandmothers were named Ida. My father's parents, Ida and Ben Singer, had two sons. My father's older brother, Irv, never married, so I was their only grandchild and, consequently, their only hope for future generations of the family in America. They were kind and loving, simple people who spoke little English and could not read or write. Ida Singer was like a little meek mouse. She had suffered a stroke at an early age, which left her with mild paralysis, unable to do many physical tasks without the help of her husband or my parents. The antithesis was my maternal grandmother, Ida Levin Cohen. My mother's mother had balls. She was married, for a second time, to a wonderful man, my step-grandfather, Nate Freeman. They lived on a farm in northern California, spoke fluent English, read the Jewish newspaper *The Forward* every day, and were up to date on current affairs. Life with them was interesting and exciting.

All four of my grandparents had originally settled in Chicago. When my mother and her sister, my aunt Estelle, got married and left home, their parents decided to move from Chicago to a place they'd heard of in California, Sonoma County: a place where socialist Jews, like themselves, had settled. They bought a chicken ranch in a small agricultural town called Petaluma and without any previous experience became chicken farmers.

I spent every summer from the time I was seven until the age of fourteen with my maternal grandparents, Ida and Nate Freeman, on their chicken ranch. Those summers made up for all the turmoil of my home life. My grandparents doted on me. In their eyes I could do no wrong, and I basked in their adoration.

In stark contrast to the privileged show biz life of Studio City, Petaluma was a farming community in the breadbasket of central California, a place where Jewish immigrants had been settling since 1864. In their native countries they had been tradesmen, tailors, bakers, shoemakers—people who worked with their hands but had never been allowed to own land. Farming was as foreign to them as everything else in America, but they banded together to help each other learn, and Petaluma was a great place to do that. Land was cheap, and organizations like the Hebrew Free Loan Society and the Jewish Agricultural Society gave aid to Jewish immigrants by offering no-interest loans to help newcomers get started. In practically no time, the Petaluma Jews became successful chicken farmers.

Petaluma was known as the Egg Capital of the World and proudly announced its claim with two huge monuments, one bearing a giant chicken and a logo that read, "THE KINGDOM OF 10,000,000 WHITE LEGHORNS—PETALUMA," and the other a rendering of an oversized basket filled with eggs reading, "PETALUMA—THE WORLD'S EGG BASKET—PRODUCES ANNUALLY 45,000,000 DOZEN EGGS." Among the locals, Petaluma had earned the nickname Chickaluma.

My grandmother Ida Levin Cohen was a no-nonsense woman who got up every day, put on her pants, and went to work feeding chickens and gathering eggs. I was in awe of her and followed her around learning how to be a tough little farm girl and to appreciate the benefits of self-reliance that comes from hard physical labor. I cleaned chicken coops and helped my grandmother feed the chickens and tend to the other farm animals. When I would feed the chickens, if I saw one that was dead, I would pick it up, sling it over my shoulder, and remove it from the flock. I never thought anything about it. It was just what you did. When my grandfather went into town to buy feed, I rode in the back of his pickup truck with their dog, Robchik. I became friends with an Italian girl, Jo, who lived across the road. Sometimes she would ride along in the truck and we would sing Everly Brothers' songs at the top of our lungs. In the afternoons when all the chores were done, I was free to play with the farm animals, including the fuzzy soft yellow baby chicks. I'd press my cheek against their downy softness and feel the pure joy of holding a tiny living creature in my hands. We also had a black and white cow and several sheep. My favorite was a gimpy little lamb named Limpy. I would bring him scraps from the dinner table, and he would nuzzle my hand and look at me with eyes so deep and sorrowful that my heart would go out to him.

I loved the farm, all the different smells and sounds. I remember it had this circular gravel driveway, and I can hear it now, the cars going up and around. In the middle of it were these giant pine trees that perfumed the air and gave a kind of majesty to my grandparents' fading gray two-story Craftsman-style house. Upstairs, where I slept, there were two bedrooms but no bathroom. The only bathroom was downstairs next to my grandparents' room. If I needed to pee in the middle of the night, I either had to tip-toe downstairs in the dark or use the chamber pot that sat by the side of my bed. I usually opted for the pot, which I had to empty in the morning. Back home, everything my mother asked me to do, from washing the dishes to making my bed, seemed like an odious chore, but here on the farm, I emptied the chamber pot and handled dead chickens and took it all in stride. I was surrounded by love, and that made all the difference.

My favorite thing of all was waking up at the crack of dawn to the mouthwatering smell of my grandmother's cinnamon rolls wafting upstairs from the kitchen. I would lie in bed breathing in the sweet aroma, anticipating the deliciousness that was to come.

Besides putting in a full day's work on the farm, my grandmother would clean the house, do the laundry, and cook three meals a day. She was a wonderful cook who made all her own breads, pastries, and even bagels. She was known for her rich, thick soups, which my grandfather would judge by testing to see whether a wooden spoon could stand straight up in the pot. And chicken? My grandmother could cook chicken a hundred different ways. My grandfather and I would go to the hen house and pick out a nice plump bird. He would tie the feet together and hang the chicken on a hook and kill it according to kosher law: slitting the throat and letting the blood drip out. It was prohibited for the blood to remain in the body of the chicken. I never thought of it as barbaric; it was just what we did. He explained to me that this was the humane way because the bird died instantly and didn't suffer. I fully accepted his explanation, and after killing the chicken in this way we would take it to my grandmother, who would pluck its feathers, clean it, and cook it. It was always delicious.

One of our neighbors had a huge vegetable garden, and we would trade a chicken for a rainbow of fresh vegetables to accompany our meal. The food was clean and fresh, with no preservatives or other toxic ingredients. Except for milk and butter and some other basics, we hardly ever had to shop at the local grocery store. One of the most enduring lessons I learned in Petaluma was self-sufficiency. Unlike city life, on the farm you could survive by your own two hands.

There was another—less obvious but very different—side to Petaluma. The Jewish immigrants who had settled there brought with them an idealistic concept of communal life built around shared political ideals and intellectual pursuits, very much like the Israeli kibbutzim. What they didn't bring was any kind of formal religious beliefs. At first, they even refused to build a synagogue, opting instead for a Jewish community center. While still remaining culturally Jewish, they wanted to avoid the dogma of organized religion. They observed the high holidays but did not adhere to any orthodoxy. Their touchstone was the teachings of great writers and philosophers. The community center was home to a drama group, a reading circle, a chorus, and numerous charitable organizations like B'nai B'rith and Hadassah, an international women's association. Here among the chickens and eggs, the immigrants created an idealistic model of communal life in America. It was a social experiment that attracted poets, writers, and speakers and inspired visits from notable Jewish leaders, including Golda Meir, Yitzhak Ben-Zvi (the president of Israel), and labor leader Harry Bridges.

In other ways, Petaluma was like many small towns across America. At the end of summer there was a big celebration of Egg Day, including a rodeo, an Egg Queen Ball, and a parade with people dressed in silly chicken costumes. On the weekends people finished their chores early and with a cry of "We're going to the river!" headed off to swim and picnic at the nearby Russian River. The Jewish community had their own spot on the river where all the women would bring home-cooked dishes to share, each woman taking pride in her special contribution. It was a day of feasting and swimming and enjoying the bounty that America had promised and delivered to hardworking immigrants.

The polar opposite of weekends on the farm were weekends when my mom would come get me in Petaluma and we would go down to San Francisco to meet my dad for a quick vacation. We'd get dressed up and go to chichi restaurants and jazz clubs, where he enjoyed the camaraderie of fellow musicians who either knew him or knew of him. It was fun to revert to my other self for a while and spend time with my father, who seemed happy and relaxed for a change.

I understood how radically different life in Petaluma was from my home life, but I accepted the dichotomy of those two worlds without question. What I didn't realize was that these two diverse experiences were setting up forces within me that would vie for control of my destiny: on the one hand, my passionate devotion to art and beauty and, on the other, my deep desire for security and stability. It would take years of experience and a lot of therapy to get these polar opposites integrated into a single well-balanced personality.

3

SURVIVING ADOLESCENCE

Yesterday I was clever and wanted to change the world. Today I am wise so I am changing myself.

—RUMI

Given the fact that I've spent so much time throughout my professional career listening to women talk about their insecurities, let me tell you a little bit more about mine.

To say that the arguments between my parents frightened me is an understatement. They terrified me. The only way I could think of to deal with this painful discord was to be even more of a "good little girl," to get straight As and Bs in school, and to be smarter than everyone else. I twisted myself into a pretzel of goodness and paid for it dearly. My recurring stomach problem now often ended with me crouched over, hugging a pillow to my stomach to ease the raging pain that no doctor could diagnose or cure. A "sensitive stomach" was the best they could come up with. No one ever considered what the cause of my condition might be.

If I had a sister or brother to talk to, I might never have needed to invent DeeGee, the imaginary friend who became my faithful childhood companion. How or when I came up with the name DeeGee is a mystery to me, and I can't recall any physical description of her, but she was a calming influence, someone I could go to when there was no one else to comfort me. If overly sensitive little Roberta Joy Singer couldn't get up off the floor, wise and funny DeeGee was always ready with a kind word to help her get back on her feet. In this convoluted way I learned I could trust my mind to help me out of a bad situation. It was a skill that I would need as I entered my teens, when all my insecurities, combined with raging hormones, sent me into a tailspin of teenage angst. My first challenge was the stutter. Fortunately, my parents put me in a special class at school, and it worked. Then, as I got a little older, my face began to break out, so much so that I had to see a dermatologist once a month for dry ice treatments. On top of that, I had to wear braces because I had buck teeth. By the time I was four-teen, I went from a 32A bra to a 32D. Boobs, zits, braces, stutter—and no siblings to protect me—made for a perfect cocktail of insecurities. And let's not forget my frizzy hair, which I had to beat into submission by putting a giant roller on top of my head, while wrapping my wet hair around my head, plastering it down with gooey Dep. I would sit under a cap hair dryer for an hour, then rewind my hair in the opposite direction and sit under the dryer all over again, until my hair was dry. Then after all the torture, I would have some semblance of decent hair. Add the fact that none of the boys wanted to date me and you'll under-stand why I wasn't a very happy camper. Worse still, I truly believed I was overweight. I scoured the fashion magazines for photos of glamor-ous models to see how I compared. Needless to say, I didn't. The dream of becoming a fashion model no longer fit my reality. It's a miracle I made it out of my teens with any degree of self-esteem.

I hated what I saw in my mirror, and despite my natural outgoing personality, I began to withdraw. I was an Energizer Bunny stuck with a lot of pent-up drive, and the only way to save myself was to focus my intense curiosity on the world around me. I collected coins and stamps and found comfort in organizing and classifying them. I would find a worm in the garden and go to the encyclopedia to identify it and learn its characteristics. When I was really bored, I would read *World Book Encyclopedia*, especially when the new edition came out each year. I built a body of factual knowledge that impressed people and brought me a measure of respect and admiration. It may have been a meager reward for the pain I was enduring, but at least it was some kind of recognition. Slowly, I began to emerge from my cocoon. I can't say I came out a beautiful butterfly, but at least I was not the ugly duckling I had believed myself to be. I had overcome the awkwardness of braces and zits, my stutter had been cured, and the rest of my body had caught up with my blooming breasts. Maybe, just maybe, I was beginning to believe that I was pretty.

By the time I was fourteen, I was surrounded by a group of girlfriends who helped build a wall of protection against my parents' battles. They still fought like crazy; they hadn't changed, but I had. I was starting to feel free of their emotional rollercoaster, and here and there I began to catch a glimpse of what my future might look like. The freedom of my teens was exciting, and my friends and I took advantage of it—not in any dangerous way, as we were not into defying our parents—but now we could ride the bus and explore the world on our own terms, no longer tethered to our mothers' apron strings. We would walk to the nearby shopping area of Ventura Boulevard to sample the 31 flavors at Baskin-Robbins or go to the movies at the local Studio City Theater or enjoy a cherry soda at the Thrifty drugstore on the corner of Ventura Boulevard and Laurel Canyon. A really big adventure was when my best friend, Sharon, and I would take the bus from Studio City to the corner of Hollywood Boulevard and

Highland Avenue. We would stroll around, eat lunch, and shop for lipsticks—preferably our favorite, Tangee Natural, a lipstick that went on clear and gradually changed color to complement your skin tone. It was advertised as "ideal for women who want to look beautiful without looking artificial." That was us! We felt so sophisticated making our beauty purchases. Then like the good little girls we were, we'd hop on a bus and return home.

When I was in the second half of tenth grade, I rushed a social club, the Corinthians. At that time, there were social clubs at most Los Angeles high schools, sort of like sororities and fraternities in college. Most of my friends wanted to be in the Corinthians. If you were lucky enough to make it, a few cars full of girls from the club would pull up in front of your house and sing the club song. I waited all day, but they never came. I was devastated. All my friends, save one, were accepted. Why not me? I never learned the answer, but I felt crushed. Then, as summer approached, I decided the reason was that I was too fat.

Maybe it had something to do with the embarrassing scene my mother once made at a birthday party. I was wearing a bathing suit, and she snatched the piece of cake I was eating and smeared it on my thigh, exclaiming, "You might as well just rub it on your thighs, cause that's where it's going to end up!" Perhaps it was her body shaming that caused my obsession. My guess is she didn't want me to wind up with the weight problem that she was constantly fighting—but whatever the reason, my thighs were a constant source of frustration and embarrassment. Why did they have to be so big? Why couldn't I have long, lean, shapely legs that looked great in a miniskirt? Why couldn't I be taller or flat-chested, like the models?

Everything was about food in our house. I mean, we had a salami hanging on the door, and I'd come home and whack off a slice and eat it. Both my mother and my aunt Estelle were overweight and continually on a diet, so I followed suit. I went on a diet and lost twenty pounds. I now weighed 100 pounds, and at 5 feet 4 inches tall, I was on the cusp of being anorexic, just like most of the models.

When I returned to school in September of 1958 for my junior year, everyone was complimenting me on my new look. I again tried to get into the Corinthians, and this time I succeeded. Subconsciously, I believed I was accepted because of my svelte figure, not wanting to believe the real truth—that my friends had simply voted me in. This was an idiotic idea that stuck with me for years before I was mature enough to accept its lunacy.

If only I could have known then that my insecurity was just a big waste of time and was keeping me from doing so many things in life, but that was a lesson that would take me a long time to learn. At my twentieth high school reunion I finally discovered that the boys actually thought I was cute and even had a clever nickname for me. They called me Body Swinger instead of Bobbe Singer. (I think my high school friend Alan Salter made this name up.) And the reason they never asked me out? They thought I was dating older guys! (It just shows what low self-esteem can do to a person's impression of how the world sees them.)

It was around that same time that my mother bought me a subscription to *Seventeen* magazine. It became my bible. My passion for detail drove me to examine every photo to discover how the models' eyes were lined, what color shadow was used, how the mascara had been applied. I pasted a picture of the actress Sophia Loren on my mirror to practice copying her look. I began to recognize certain tricks that made her eyes pop and sparkle. I started fooling around with my mother's makeup and realized that my mother had the worst makeup. She had a green and a blue shadow stick where, after you blinked your eyes four times, you'd get lines all over your eyelids; lipsticks that were unattractive; and caked powder and blushes that were ugly. I started really looking into how products were made, and I prowled the makeup counters at department stores while studying the different brands and the myriad options there were for creating a "look." Little by little I would ask my mother, "Can I go get this? Can I go get that?" I began gathering the products I needed, and I started doing my own makeup. I wasn't thinking about it as a career; it was just something I enjoyed doing for myself. Sometimes I would even help out one of my girlfriends when she was going to prom or out on a date.

What fascinated me most was that there was an artistic component to the application of makeup. I could see how the same model with a different lipstick or a different eyeliner could become a different person. I was at that vulnerable age where we were all trying to figure out who we were, and if I could enhance my eyes or accentuate my lips or shape my brows, it was like making myself into someone else.

I was beginning to recognize that I had inherited some of my mother's artistic talent, and this was an exciting way to put it to use. Little did I know I was starting on a path that would become my life's passion.

The Singer family home in Studio City right after a freak snowstorm, 1949. The house that music built

(L-R) My paternal grandparents, Grandpa Ben Singer and Grandma Ida Singer; Uncle Irving Singer; and my father, Lou Singer, circa 1927

(L-R) My favorite aunt Estelle Saks, my mother's sister; my uncle Harold Saks; Mom; cousin August Lowenstein; and my maternal grandmother, Nanny Ida, in Chicago in the early 1940s

Playing the bass drum at the age of 3. Before we moved to Studio City from Griffith Park

Celebrating my fourth or fifth birthday

For Purim, I'm dressed as Queen Esther. Central Casting?

21

*My mother, Nanny (my mother's mother); my cousin
Nancy; Grandpa Nate; and me on the farm, 1953*

Nanny, Nancy, and me in front of the house in Petaluma

My grandpa Nate Freeman on
his chicken ranch in Petaluma,
California, 1955. It was my
safe and happy place.

Feeding the cow on my grandfather's farm, 1953

23

Limpy the lamb with me and my friend Jo, 1953

4

UP AND DOWN

Don't look back; you're not going that way.

—AUTHOR UNKNOWN

When I was fifteen, I became confident enough in my looks to take a course at the highly respected Mary Webb Davis Modeling Agency in Hollywood. Her office was on Sunset Boulevard next to the famed Dino's Lounge, owned by the singer Dean Martin. It was 1959, and the hit television series that year was *77 Sunset Strip.* In the opening credits the camera panned across a shot of Dino's Lounge and the front doors of the Mary Webb Davis Modeling Agency. Walking through those doors made me feel like I was already part of something special.

My years of going to department store runway shows with my mother and practicing my modeling poses in front of the mirror, plus the countless hours of soaking up details in fashion magazines, put me way ahead of the game. I came to class stylishly dressed with my hair and makeup done to a tee. I knew I was at the top of my class.

Mary Webb Davis was caring and kind; she was also a no-nonsense, straightforward woman. At the end of my course, I eagerly approached her, asking for advice on what the next step should be in my modeling career. Secretly, I believed that she had already recognized my skills and would sign me as a client with her agency. Instead, she looked me over with a wry smile and said, "Unless you're going to grow another five inches, I'm afraid you're not going to be a fashion model." My face must have fallen to the floor. She softened her tone and looked me squarely in the eyes and said, "It doesn't matter how pretty or how talented you are; modeling is a business for tall women. That's just how it is." Sometimes it takes a bucket of cold water to help you see the truth. I might as well have dreamed of being a Sumo wrestler or an Olympic hurdler. Accepting who we are is an essential step toward discovering who we are meant to be. Just like that, my dream of a modeling career ended. *Que sera, sera.*

Once I graduated from North Hollywood High, it was a given that I would attend college. My very liberal Petaluma grandparents, who unfortunately were no longer alive, had been eager for me to attend the University of California at Berkeley (CAL), a top-ranked and suitably liberal university. I had no real criteria for judging colleges, but I loved my grandparents, and even after their deaths I was still seeking their approval. I wasn't really sure what I would major in, but I had a good ear and an interest in foreign languages. So, at seventeen, having convinced myself that Berkeley was where I wanted to go, I left home for CAL as a foreign-language major.

Neither of my parents had attended college, so I was somewhat in the dark as to how it all worked. It was my first time alone away from home and my first time sharing a room with someone else. I was very insecure as to how to fit in. On the political side, it was a wonderful experience: students on soapboxes, protesting just about everything. I joined the Peace and Freedom Party and loved taking the bus into San Francisco from Berkeley to mingle with the hippies who crowded the streets. Great music and art were coming out of San Francisco, and I enjoyed being a part of it.

My roommate was nice enough, but we had absolutely nothing in common. I had trouble relating to a lot of the girls in my dorm. I was very lonely. I'd always been a good student, but now I found myself struggling. There were almost a thousand students in the lecture halls. Everything was so impersonal; the best I could do was figure out how much information I could possibly memorize.

During my first semester I came down with the flu, and they stuck me in the hospital so I wouldn't infect everyone in the dorm. I missed my midterms, and my grades ended up being two Bs, a D, and an F. I had never seen a D or an F on any of my report cards until then. The stress just kept building until, finally, I realized that UC Berkeley wasn't the right place for me. Even though I tested well academically, Berkeley was too intense, too political. I needed a more relaxed, creative atmosphere.

Ultimately, anxiety completely overtook me. I felt as if I was a total failure. Reluctantly, I called my mother. From the tone of my voice, she knew immediately that I was at my wits' end and that I was close to a nervous breakdown. She and my aunt Estelle flew up to Berkeley, and before the school year was out, they brought me home.

My aunt Estelle was my mother's younger sister, by eight years. I was grateful to see her arrive in Berkeley. In my constant desire for siblings I viewed my aunt Estelle as a big sister. She was a confidante who often cushioned the blows between me and my mother. She had three children of her own, including my closest cousin, Nancy, but Aunt Estelle was always there for me when I needed a warm embrace or comforting advice.

Back home with my parents, I struggled to find my footing. My best friends were at colleges all over the country and seemed to be succeeding. I still had ambitions to graduate from a major university, so I enrolled in summer school at USC, where I earned the kind of grades I was used to. I was beginning to feel like myself again.

• • •

In the 1960s, Palm Springs was the place to go for spring break or any other holiday. "The Springs" offered an opportunity to get away from the boredom of our home lives and "live a little." We'd all flock to a motel in Palm Springs, with one of the parents in tow as a chaperone, and end up splashing in a pool with some guys we'd never met before.

That's how I met my first husband. I was eighteen and thought he was cute. He wanted to be a lawyer—I was impressed. We started dating, and it soon became known that we were a couple. I liked having a steady boyfriend; it gave me the kind of grounding I needed. I had been doing well at USC, but my boyfriend was going to Cal State Northridge (CSUN), so with very little hesitation I transferred there.

At CSUN, I was pleasantly surprised to find the kind of creative atmosphere I was looking for. I had a jazz class there that was beyond anything I'd ever taken. I took a criminology class led by the man who started Synanon, the first important drug rehabilitation program in the US. He would bring in former drug addicts to talk to us, and I felt I was getting a real experience. I wasn't just memorizing bullshit that I was never going to use, which is what I felt I was doing at Berkeley. It was great to be in a place where I felt safe and comfortable, though I must admit it was as if I was back in high school. Maybe that was the real problem all along; I needed people around me who made me feel secure.

I may have resolved my immediate problems, but it didn't mean I had conquered my insecurities. No, in fact, they were still very much in control and still driving me to make some very questionable decisions in my life.

All my friends were getting engaged or married, and I didn't want to be left out, so my boyfriend and I decided to get married. It was the one time I should have paid closer attention to my father. When I told him I was getting married, his reaction was, "So?" He wasn't impressed. Nevertheless, he and my mother threw us a big Jewish wedding attended by many of my father's friends in the music business, including the famous Borscht Belt clarinetist and comedian Mickey Katz. The International Hotel at LAX had just opened, and it had a grand ballroom, big enough to hold our hundred and fifty guests, who were all attired in tuxedos and evening gowns. I wore a white lace fitted sheath with a detachable satin train. The dress clung to all my curves, and my bridesmaids wore flowing pink empire-waist gowns and headbands with little veils attached. It was beautiful—a dream wedding. Too bad the marriage didn't last.

I've been unprepared for many things in life, but none of them compared with how unprepared I was for marriage. Both my new husband and I agreed that the most important thing was for him to get his law degree, and, of course, he couldn't work while he was studying full time. So it was my wifely duty to put him through law school. In 1964 my college life came to an abrupt end. I dropped out of school and started looking for work. I never questioned the appropriateness of this decision or how it might affect my future earning potential. I put all my hopes and dreams aside for my husband, in the same way that my mother sacrificed herself for my father's career.

Both my parents and my husband's parents did help us out, but I needed to work, so I took any kind of job I could get. I worked in a bank as a teller, I worked in an office at Universal Studios, and I even got a job at the famed Hollywood makeup company Max Facto where my duties consisted of typing copy for ads. I remember hating every minute of it, because you had to put carbon paper in between the sheets, and every time you made a mistake—"Oh, please, no! Oh my God!" It was horrible!

I floundered from job to job. All I knew was that I had to support my husband. He was our hope for the future; he would be our bread-winner, and my role was to be the good little wife who would take care of everything until then. It never dawned on me that I might be heading down the same destructive path that my mother had followed. But I would soon find out.

As long as we are on my insecurities, let me tell you about one of my most difficult ones. My aunt Estelle had three children, Nancy, Richard, and David. Nancy was two years younger than I, and, being an only child myself, I was thrilled to have this "sister-like" relationship with her. She was my maid of honor at my wedding, even though she was not enamored of my husband—and showed it in some not-so-nice ways.

I loved her with all my heart, but I could see the handwriting on the wall. When she entered college, she rebelled, not only against me but also against the entire family. At one point she got pregnant and thought nothing of coming to me with her problem. I had just had my son, Ian, so I guess she thought I would be the one who could help her out. And I did.

Through someone I knew, I was able to find a doctor who came to my apartment and performed an abortion on this twenty-year-old cousin I loved. I cared for her and took her to my gynecologist the next day to make sure everything was all right. Done. Problem

and even though she remained quite rebel-
earn a BS and her MSW and was working as

29

a therapist. One would think that perhaps that might clue her in to her issues with the family, but it took years for her to come around. She was in and out of my life, and sometimes it felt like I was on an emotional rollercoaster. Therapy for me was packed with Nancy stories and my hurt feelings.

When my uncle, her dad, was dying, she came back into the fold. We somewhat rekindled our relationship, and one night while at dinner together she asked me whether I knew that she had had an abortion. At this point she was forty, and I was forty-two. I looked at her totally astonished and reminded her of my involvement in that experience. I'm not sure where she had stored that memory away or how I had been left out of it—but, again, it was hurtful.

Anytime she didn't like something that I said or did, she would cease talking to me, for years at a time. And, believe me, it was for the dumbest things. She proceeded to get a PhD in psychology, but her ability to assess the damage she did to those around her was nil.

Then, sadly, I learned she was diagnosed with breast cancer. I called her to see what I could do, if I could help her find a wig or anything. She was thankful. The next day, she called to ask me not to tell anyone, as she didn't want her clients to know. I told her that I wouldn't but that I had to tell my children, who were now adults, because our grandmother, my aunt (her mother), and now my cousin had all inherited the BRCA gene mutation, which makes us more susceptible to breast cancer. I felt it was important for our family to know and be able to put it on their medical records.

Then, suddenly, she stopped talking to me again. By then I was through. I had suffered with this nonsense most of my life. I was now in my sixties, and I was done. I was hurt and saddened because this brilliant, pretty, accomplished woman who had meant so much to me couldn't even be my friend.

A year or so went by, and one day I received a note in the mailbox. It said the following: "I'm sorry if I did anything to hurt you. Nancy." Just like that. Nothing more. I never spoke to her after receiving the note, and, sadly, she died soon after from a massive heart attack. I felt the loss as a terrible gaping hole, a piece of unfinished business in my life.

Closure finally came when my aunt said to me, "You know, Nancy was always jealous of you." I had loved her so much that I never thought of that possibility—but it certainly explained everything and was the closure that I needed.

Funny how we can allow someone else to be responsible for our feelings.

5

A LIFE-CHANGING
ENCOUNTER

*You're braver than you believe and stronger than
you seem and smarter than you think.*

—A. A. MILNE

In 1964, Beatlemania swept America, and I, like everyone
else, was caught in the frantic adoration of four "mop-top" boys whose
look included a messy haircut that ended the slicked-back style of the
1950s. Hair became a symbol of rebellion. When it came to fashion,
I was always on the cutting edge, and I heard about a hair stylist at
the Bill White Salon in nearby Encino in the San Fernando Valley
who was doing fabulous cuts for all the trendy people in Hollywood.
His name was Jon Peters, and I wanted the look he was turning out. I
immediately booked an appointment. When I arrived, the receptionist
pointed him out. "That's him over there," she said, nodding toward
a handsome young dark-haired boy who looked to be no more than
eighteen or nineteen. He was wielding a blow-dryer and putting the
finishing touches on the feathered mane of a somewhat familiar-
looking blonde starlet. I watched with fascination as he stepped back

and admired his own work. The blonde slipped him a gratuity, and he kissed her on both cheeks. Then with a last flip of his fingers through her hair and a pat on her bottom, he sent her off feeling great about herself. I was awestruck and a little intimidated by this playful and charismatic charmer, until the moment I sat down in his chair. He took one look at me and said, "I know you. You're Roberta Singer, and you were in Miss Cunningham's class at Dixie Canyon Avenue."

"What?" It took me a moment to recognize him. "Oh yeah. You're the boy who was in the principal's office all the time."

"Yeah," he said in a sexy, pompous way, "that's me."

"But wasn't your name Jon Bairo?"

"That was my stepfather's name. Now I go by Jon Peters, my real name."

He sized me up with a swift glance. "Looking good, Singer. You married?"

"Almost a year. How about you?"

"Yep."

He leaned in close and whispered in my ear, "I'm about to open my own beauty salon. Wanna be my receptionist?"

It was a bit too much, too soon. I declined.

"Thanks. But, actually, I already have a job."

While he snipped away at my hair, I couldn't help comparing my frustrating carbon-copy life at Max Factor with the freewheeling energy of the beauty salon. At the end of our appointment I definitely walked out feeling good about myself and my new haircut but also feeling some regret about having rejected his offer.

I was never what you'd call a regular beauty salon customer. I had gone occasionally with my mother when it was still referred to as the beauty shop. That's when salons were old school—lots of women seated under turban-sized metal hairdryers, smoking and reading

Ladies' Home Journal. Things had changed drastically in the past few years.

By the time I was ready for another haircut, the new Jon Peters Salon had opened in Encino, very near my house. Already there was a lot of buzz about it. Jon just seemed to know how to generate excitement. I was eager to see the new space, so I made an appointment with him and instantly liked what I saw.

The new salon was filled with hip young people; rock and roll music played over the sound system, and there was nothing old-fashioned about it. Even the design of the salon was avant-garde, with a special glass cubicle where Jon was set apart from the other stylists but still visible—as if he were onstage performing his hair magic. There was a vibe to the place that was contagious, and it was obvious that the clients and the stylists were all having a great time.

Jon seemed truly happy to see me and pleaded in a boyish voice, "Bobbe, please, please, come work here. I need a receptionist, and you'd be so good!" I was ready, he was charming, I capitulated.

I told my husband that I was quitting my secure secretarial job at Max Factor in order to be a receptionist in a start-up hair salon, and he got very excited. He loved the notion that I would be rubbing shoulders with celebrities and "happening" people. He had been a cheerleader in high school and could easily see himself fitting right in with that crowd. His next question was how much more money I would make. What he really cared about was whether I was going to make enough to continue supporting him as he slogged his way through law school. I assured him I would.

Life at the salon was a blast. Jon was always kidding around and set the tone for the whole salon by being edgy and silly. Sometimes he could needle you or even be a little nasty, but it always in fun. The other stylists picked up on Jon's brashness and followed his example.

One of the stylists was the very talented Allen Edwards, who created the famous Farrah Fawcett haircut and would later go on to open his own chain of successful hair salons. One of the other stylists was Jon's business partner, Paul Canter. He was attractive, in a Tom Jones kind of way, with dark curly hair, and he was more businesslike than Jon. He seemed a little stand-offish to me, and for some reason I got the feeling that he didn't really like me, but we got along well enough, mainly because he respected my contribution to the salon.

I must admit I was very good at my job. I had the right kind of friendly, outgoing personality it takes to hold down the front desk, which often got crazy with booking appointments, interacting with the clients, and making sure the stylists were kept on track with all their bookings. Part of my job was to personify the salon's "hip" style. I felt lucky to have a job where my sense of fashion was the required dress code. I tried out all kinds of looks, everything from funky San Francisco/hippie to the British elegance of Jean Shrimpton (my favorite model, whom some people thought I resembled). Nothing I could wear was too far out for this crowd; they were on the cutting edge of everything, and it was a great practice ground for developing my own style.

The women who came to the salon all wanted to get "that look," whatever the look of the day was. It could be either the Vidal Sassoon very geometric cut or the sexy, fluffy look that Jon was so good at. I loved seeing the clients strut out with that extra little zing that a new haircut can give you. It reinforced my belief that taking care of yourself and looking good weren't just vanity. They had real emotional and psychological benefits.

As time went on, Jon added other cool perks to the salon: a jewelry counter that sold earthy, funky turquoise jewelry and another that sold high-priced gold and diamond pieces. He brought in a woman named Monique Chic, who had her own line of cosmetics and offered makeup services for the clients. It was all part of his out-of-the-box thinking. When people came to the Jon Peters Salon, he wanted them to have a unique experience.

I was extremely interested in what Monique had to offer, but after seeing the results of her makeup on various clients, it seemed dated—as if she was stuck in my mother's generation. In 1965, Twiggy, a fifteen-year-old anorexic from England, became the new face of beauty. She stunned the fashion world with her dramatic eye makeup, spikey lashes, and futuristic hairstyle, and instantly I knew that was a direction I wanted to go in. I was quick to emulate Twiggy, and everybody took notice.

"What are you wearing on your eyes?" they asked. "That's so cool. How do you do that?"

I greatly appreciated their admiration, and I began to believe that makeup was something I had a special talent for. The idea that I could make a career of it hadn't yet occurred to me. Even if it had, I wouldn't have had a clue how to go about it. There wasn't a school; nobody gave makeup lessons. I wouldn't even have known where to start. I was happy to stay at the front desk, put on my wardrobe and makeup du jour, and be a part of the lively show at the Jon Peters Salon.

When I first started working there, I was still a very good little girl. My big attempt at sophistication was smoking cigarettes. I knew that some people were starting to cross into riskier territory—smoking pot, taking pills—but this was never something I wanted to do. I was afraid of drugs and wary of some of the behavior that was becoming the hallmark of the "happening scene."

On that fateful day when Jon and I reconnected at Bill White's hair salon, we were basically still children—children who were already married. Jon was nineteen; his young bride, Marie, was about my age, twenty; and my husband was twenty-two. We were all in a big rush to make our mark and to own the world, but Jon went at it with more gusto than anyone else. His status as a rising star, combined with an excess of adoration from all the beautiful young women who surrounded him, caused problems in his marriage, and in a short time he and Marie divorced. They remained friends, but Jon became a serial dater, and rumors about his wild sexual adventures became the titillating gossip of the salon.

One day, while I was working at the reception desk, the phone rang. It was a girl who insisted on speaking to Jon. I buzzed his private room.

"There's a Suzy on the phone for you." I could see him in his glass cage, scissors in hand, executing a feathered cut on a head of long dark hair.

He shouted back over the speaker, "Suzy who?"

"She didn't give a last name," I replied.

Without missing a beat, he responded, "Ask her if she's the one I fucked last night."

I stammered, "I'm . . . I'm not going to ask her that!"

Jon came out of his private room and pointed his scissors at me.

"Ask her!" he ordered with a devilish grin.

By now the whole salon was staring at us. I shook my head defiantly as tears welled in my eyes. Then he laughed and took the call. It wasn't easy working for Jon. Deep down I still believed that manners and breeding mattered, and I couldn't always go along with Jon's crazy ways.

●　●　●

Most Saturdays Jon didn't want to take the day's cash receipts home with him because he would be heading straight from the salon to a night on the town with his next stunning conquest. At that time my husband and I lived in Encino. Our apartment was about five minutes from the salon, so I was in charge of taking the cash home with me. On Sunday mornings Jon would come by to get the money, with whatever girl he had been with the night before hanging on his arm. Miniskirts were the fashion, and young hot starlets, their eye makeup still smudged from the previous night, would appear with Jon at our apartment dressed in their minis with no panties on, flashing a "Sharon Stone," much to the entertainment of my husband. Jon loved to shock, to say the least.

Then, to all our surprise, in 1967 Jon ended his exhaustive dating binge by marrying Lesley Ann Warren, a very talented and success-ful young television and film actress. She was from a Russian/Jewish background, just like me. I thought, "Wow, Jon found a nice Jewish girl: sweet, smart, talented, and more grown-up than the others."

They settled down in a lovely home in Sherman Oaks, and I remember being invited to their house for a Saturday night party. In my mind I pictured the kind of get-together my parents often had with their friends: a relaxed evening of eating, drinking, kids playing, everyone civilized and social. Was I ever mistaken!

Jon and Lesley Ann's party was loaded with celebrities, friends, and even some family members, including Jon's wild and crazy cousin Silvio. It was the beginning of the naked pool parties, and over in one corner a girl was slowly letting her top fall away from her body while in another corner a star was sniffing coke with her boyfriend. As I turned to say something to my husband, I saw Jon's cousin Silvio standing on his head, naked, with his penis staring me in the face. I felt like I was in a Fellini movie. It was freedom, it was youth, it was "sex, drugs, and rock 'n' roll," and Jon Peters was our ringleader.

To some degree we all fell under Jon's spell. All the time I was working as a receptionist, I was also a guinea pig for Jon. He would constantly change the color and style of my hair. I was a redhead, a blonde, a brunette. I had highlights, long hair to my shoulders, a short bob. Whatever Jon was interested in at the moment he would try out on me. And like a good little girl, I let him.

One morning after I had been working at the salon for almost a year, I woke up feeling sick. I pushed myself to go to work, thinking it was a flare-up of my old stomach issues. But the following morning I was so nauseated that I thought I was going to throw up. I decided to see my doctor. His diagnosis? I was pregnant. I was excited, terrified, and confused. I didn't know whether it was the beginning of something wonderful or the end of a lifestyle I was just beginning to enjoy. Since there was no way of knowing the answer, I decided it would be best not to think about it and to continue working through my entire pregnancy.

In my ninth month Jon decided he should cut my hair like Mia Farrow's and bleach it blonde. It was a disaster. I had this giant round belly with a pinhead of blonde hair. I hated it. I couldn't look at myself in the mirror without bursting into tears. Immediately, I ordered a blonde fall that attached to the top of my head and hung down my back, giving the impression of long hair. I secured it with a scarf and had the pixie bangs in front and the blonde fall in back and vowed that as soon as I had my baby, I would have the fall and my hair dyed back to brown. I didn't want anyone, especially my baby, to see me looking so awful. Naturally, Jon thought the whole thing was very funny.

6

SINK OR SWIM

You might be one person to the world but you may also be the world to one person.

—AUDREY HEPBURN

In 1967, at the age of twenty-two, I gave birth to a beautiful boy we named Ian. He was a perfect baby and brought a whole new dimension to our lives. Suddenly, I understood my parents' desire to protect me from all the dangers of the world. That was exactly how I felt looking into the eyes of this little helpless creature who was completely dependent on me. Once again, I was totally unprepared. I remember driving home from the hospital with him, swaddled in his blue blanket, and asking myself, "What do I do now?" I hadn't a clue how to change a diaper, I had never been around newborn infants, and they certainly didn't come with an instruction manual. Never having had siblings didn't help either. I was in unchartered territory.

Naturally, my parents were thrilled with their grandson, and they generously offered to make a down payment on a large house for our growing family. My husband and I eagerly accepted their offer, and now we had a baby and a five-bedroom house. On the surface everything seemed to have changed, yet some things were predictably the same. My husband was still in law school, and I was still the main source of income. A few months after I gave birth to Ian, it became clear that I was going to have to go back to work—and soon.

In my brief time at home with Ian, I thought a lot about what I really wanted to do with my life and my work. I knew it wasn't going back to the reception desk. The idea of learning how to be a makeup artist had captivated my imagination, and I thought the least I could do was investigate the possibilities. Fortunately, between my mother and my mother-in-law I had plenty of babysitting help. I took advantage of both of their availability.

I don't know where I got the courage, but one morning after dropping Ian off at my mother-in-law's, I walked into the Aida Grey Salon in Beverly Hills. I had learned about Aida Grey, the great classy lady of the cosmetics world, from the sophisticated women I met in the Jon Peters Salon, and I was determined to work for her. She had the highest-quality skin care and makeup line in the US. Her clients were rich and famous, but she kept a low profile, never profiting or playing off their names. Aida Grey was from Sweden, and her Scandinavian beauty regimen included deep cleansing facials and organic skin care products long before we were all aware of what "organic" even meant. Her natural-looking foundations were specially mixed for her clientele, and her status in the world of beauty was beyond reproach.

So there I was, dressed in a fashionable print minidress with my hair and makeup done in my best Jean Shrimpton look, asking the stylish young woman at the reception desk if I could speak with Miss Aida Grey. Before I had time to realize how nervous I was, she appeared, a lovely woman in her fifties with flawless skin and bright eyes. She listened respectfully to my timid request. "I want to learn all about makeup, and I was hoping you might be willing to teach me."

She asked me a few questions, looked me up and down, and made me a surprising offer. "Find a beauty salon that you would like to set yourself up in and I'll provide you with all the products you'll need to get started." It was an overwhelming proposal. I was flattered but taken aback. I left with mixed emotions. I didn't think I knew enough to embark on such an ambitious venture. Obviously, I had impressed Aida Grey enough that she would put her trust in me—that was a big ego boost—but it didn't get me any closer to my goal. I needed a mentor, someone who would take me by the hand and walk me through the process. Sadly, I had to acknowledge that as flattering as Aida Grey's offer was, it was not right for me.

My fallback option was Monique Chic, the makeup woman at Jon Peters Salon. I didn't have as much admiration for her as I did for Aida Grey, but I gave her a call, and she said, "Absolutely, you can come here. I'll teach you everything ... blah, blah, blah." She didn't teach me much of anything! As it turned out, she was opening another makeup counter at another salon, and it worked out perfectly for her because she needed someone to handle her makeup clients at Jon Peters. Monique was aware that everyone at the salon knew me because I had been the desk girl, and many of them admired how I did my own makeup. Monique assumed, just like Aida Grey, that I would figure it out as I went along. At least in this setting I was familiar with the clientele. Despite my trepidations I accepted her offer.

So there I was, once again, on my own not knowing exactly what to do. Fortunately, the clients seemed happy to see me.

"Hi, Bobbe, so glad you're back. Oh, you're doing eyebrows. Could you do mine?"

At first I made excuses.

"I hope you'll understand I'm just learning."

"Please! Anything you do would be better than what I do."

It was like getting thrown into the deep end of the pool: you either sink or swim. I swam. The first thing I did was study the makeup products Monique had left me. Little by little I learned which foundations were best for which types of skin, which eye shadows worked with which eye colors, and how to use different eye liners and lip pencils. My clients began to trust me. Before long many of them were asking me to do their eyebrows.

Eyebrow waxing, which basically rips out unwanted hairs, had become very popular. Most eyebrow shapes harkened back to the thinly penciled Jean Harlow look of the 1930s. I thought it made women look dated and old-fashioned. My version was much more contoured. I never waxed; I only tweezed, plucking the hairs individually. It was more labor intensive, but it gave women a softer, more natural look and was much more youthful looking. I had to beg people not to make their eyebrows thin because you only have so many years in which your hair grows. After a while it just stops growing in the same way. Even I have areas where I have to fill in my eyebrows because they don't grow anymore. As my career progressed, the shaping and styling of beautiful, natural-looking eyebrows became my signature.

* * *

Once I settled into Monique's beauty counter and was comfortable with the products, things began to escalate rapidly. One afternoon, Herb Budoff, one of the salon stylists, took me aside to tell me that he was opening his own salon, the Ladies' Room, in the San Fernando Valley, with a female partner. He suggested that I come with him and create my own line of cosmetics. I wasn't too crazy about the name of the salon, but the idea of creating my own makeup line . . . well, that got my attention.

"How would I do that?" I asked.

His answer: "You'll figure it out."

I had already decided that the line of makeup Monique had left me was not really in sync with the times, and I had been thinking a lot about what I would do differently. Now this was my chance to dive into an aspect of makeup product development that I was eager to experience. I agreed to join Herb and his partner when they opened two months later. In the meantime, I would research every product I might need and create the packaging to make it look exciting.

There's nothing like a deadline to get you going. I was on a roll. I started going to makeup shows, and I ripped the names of manufacturers and distributors out of the Yellow Pages and visited them in person. That's where I discovered something very surprising. The same people who created the products for the big-name companies sold exactly the same products to all the smaller companies, who basically got the benefit of the research that had been paid for by the big-name brands. A new company like mine could pick and choose from items already created, put my own personal label on them, and be in business overnight. But I wanted more than to just be a copycat. I wanted my line to be something special.

From the manufacturers I learned that the difference between a lesser and higher quality of eye shadow was the amount of pigment used. More pigment in a product cost more but gave a richer color. I learned how to select the foundations that were less likely to cake and how the various ingredients in lipsticks were what gave them their specific qualities: glossy, matte, color, aroma, etc.

I wanted my line of products to be ranked with the best, so I started with the highest quality I could find, and when I wasn't happy with a product, I learned how to make it better. It was truly a creative and inventive time for me, and I felt the deep-down satisfaction of seeing my ideas come to life by my own two hands. It was the same feeling I had experienced on my grandparents' chicken farm, a feeling of honest work that made me feel deeply connected to my true self. And then I realized that was the feeling I had been striving for all along. I knew then I was on the right track.

Despite all the glamour associated with makeup, developing my personal line was a hands-on process that literally started in my kitchen. All my friends and family were pressed into service, pasting on labels, doing inventory, and, later on, hand tying eyelashes.

The next big challenge was finding a name for my products. I looked at all the other cosmetic lines, and for the most part they were named after the head of the company (Revlon, Elizabeth Arden, Aida Grey) or sometimes a family member (Maybelline, Estée Lauder). My middle name was Joy, and I wanted my products to bring happiness into people's lives, so I named the product Bobbe Joy. I had inherited enough of my mother's artistic talent to create an attractive design that would be used for my labels and marketing, and the satisfaction of pasting that first label onto the first tube of foundation was beyond anything I could have imagined.

By the time Herb Budoff's new salon was ready to open, I had my products ready to go. In 1967 I opened Bobbe's Beauty Bar in the Ladies' Room Salon and presented my makeup line, Bobbe Joy, to the world.

In fewer than six months I had gone from being a new mother to becoming a makeup artist with her own personal line of products. While it may have all seemed well calculated, the truth was I was making it up as I went along. It was the 1960s, and that's what we were all doing—not just in our careers but also in our personal lives.

7

"IF IT FEELS GOOD, DO IT"

You're always with yourself so you might as well enjoy the company

—DIANE VON FÜRSTENBERG

In the early 1970s that catchy phrase "If it feels good, do it!" served as a pop slogan for a generation committed to overturning all social norms. The Beatles' anthem "All You Need Is Love" provided the rallying cry, and young people worldwide joined the parade. I was marching somewhere along the sidelines, with one foot in the hippie revolution and the other in the world of marriage and responsibility. My personal dilemma was best captured in the 1969 movie *Bob & Carol & Ted & Alice,* about two couples who grew up during the Eisenhower years and wanted to be modern but were still hung up by their conventional values. That was me.

Navigating those two diverse paths was incredibly challenging, but in that heady time everything seemed possible, and with the great surge toward female liberation, we believed women could do it all. The trickiest notion of the time was free love, which allowed our generation to indulge in all kinds of permissive behavior and to send the societal norms spinning out of control.

The launching of Bobbe's Beauty Bar came at exactly the right moment in time. If everything was about "feeling good," then what could make you feel better than looking good? Our opening at the Ladies' Room really took off. Customers loved the Bobbe Joy makeup line, and in our first month we sold $1,000 worth of products and services, far exceeding our expectations. Herb Budoff and his partner threw a launch party, inviting all their salon pals, including Jon Peters and Paul Canter. Paul attended; Jon did not. That didn't surprise me.

When I told Jon that I was leaving to start my own business at Herb's new salon, he was seriously pissed. Jon was known to be a little over the top, but he even went so far as to accuse me of stealing from Monique. I was no newcomer to verbal abuse, but his accusation of stealing was a knife to my heart. If there was anything I took pride in, it was my honesty. I truly believe that everything you put out in the world comes back to you, and I would never incur that kind of karmic debt. I said what I had to say in my own defense, but it fell on deaf ears, and Jon and I parted on very bad terms.

His partner, Paul Canter, was far more understanding and expressed his admiration for my new Bobbe's Beauty Bar setup. He even asked how my business was doing. It was the first time he had shown any interest in me, and I proudly told him about my first month's sales. I could see he was impressed, and I secretly hoped he would pass the information back to Jon.

Even though my sales were great, not everything was going well at the Ladies' Room. There was a certain amount of tension between Herb and his partner, which I attributed to the stress of opening any new venture. I rationalized that, in time, things would work out, but the thought did cross my mind: what if they didn't? The mere prospect that I would be stuck with all my product and no place to sell it was too troublesome to contemplate. I closed my eyes and said a little prayer that everything would be OK.

One afternoon I was at my mother's when the phone rang. It was for me. It was Jon Peters. As my mother handed me the phone, my first thought was, "How did he find me here?" But knowing Jon, I figured he could track you down anywhere.

"Bobbe," he said in a very apologetic tone, "I'm really sorry for the way things ended."

"Me, too, Jon."

"Listen, I just heard that Herb and his partner aren't getting along well and he may be pulling out."

I caught my breath. That was it, the affirmation of my worst fears. "Oh, really?" I said, trying to act calm.

"Yeah, and Paul tells me you've got a nice setup there. How would you like to bring your Bobbe's Beauty Bar to the Jon Peters Salon?"

If Jon was anything, he was direct. I took a moment before answering.

"You've already got Monique there."

"I'll get rid of her," he replied. "You know, we're gonna be opening two more salons, one in Woodland Hills and one in Beverly Hills. You could end up in all three."

Jon certainly knew how to sprinkle the fairy dust, but now I was in the driver's seat and played it cool.

"Let me think about it, Jon. I'll get back to you."

"Don't take too long, Bobbe. I might change my mind."

There's something about childhood friends. No matter how mad you get at them, they hold a special place in your heart, and it's hard to let them go. The next day I had a serious talk with Herb Budoff, who confirmed that his deal at the Ladies' Room wasn't working out and he was pulling out. That meant the whole enterprise could fall apart.

That did it. Two weeks later I returned to the Jon Peters Encino Salon and set up the new Bobbe's Beauty Bar. Once there, I learned that there was more to the story of Jon's apology. Word had gotten around about the new Bobbe Joy makeup line, and many of his clients had been considering moving over to where I was or were pressuring Jon to bring me back. Knowing all that made my return even more gratifying.

Working with my own products meant I was free to tailor them to each client. I mixed individual foundations and found unique colors; I designed personal palettes and gave every client a facial map instructing them how to use the products on their own face. Everyone loved it; the products were practically selling themselves. When the Jon Peters Salon opened in Woodland Hills, I set up the second Bobbe's Beauty Bar. I was now splitting my days between Encino and Woodland Hills, and in no time it was becoming more than I could handle. Between raising my son, creating the products, servicing two salons, running a household, and keeping my husband in law school, I could see I was on the verge of becoming overwhelmed.

My near nervous meltdown in college had given me a good warning mechanism, and I knew that stressful situations could trigger my bouts of stomach cramps and heart arrhythmia. Taking care of myself was key to my well-being. It was time to hire some help.

I put the word out that I was looking for an assistant, and some truly talented young people applied. The first one I hired for the Encino salon was a beautiful girl named Eugenia Weston. She was young, eager, artistic, and great with clients. I didn't just hire Eugenia; I trained her. Unlike the women I had approached for instruction in my early years, I was willing to share all my knowledge, including everything I knew about products, skin types, facial structure, color, balance, and, most importantly, how to work with the myriad personalities that are part of the makeup world. Eugenia was the beginning of a long line of makeup artists whom I would train and launch on careers that went far beyond Bobbe's Beauty Bar. Many of them went on to develop their own makeup lines, including Eugenia, who became the founder of the Senna Cosmetics brand. At the same time, I encouraged their individual creativity, and in turn they became my faithful sidekicks. With their help I was able to keep Bobbe's Beauty Bar running smoothly and to keep my stress level under control.

• • •

From the very beginning, Jon's Encino salon attracted a Hollywood crowd. Encino, with its rolling lawns and spacious homes, was a favorite bedroom community for celebrities who wanted a more secluded lifestyle. Notable film, TV, and recording artists such as the Jackson 5, Annette Funicello, Steve Allen, Johnny Carson, Clark Gable, and Johnny Cash all had homes in Encino, along with an abundance of up-and-coming young actors and actress who were regulars at the Jon Peters Salon. Before long, some of these soon-to-be stars began asking me to do their makeup for special events: a film premiere, a Grammy red carpet appearance, or a date with a new someone. I enjoyed the challenge of tailoring their makeup to match their outfit or hairstyle, and when I watched them on TV, walking the red carpet, I took great pride in knowing that I had helped them achieve their beautiful look.

Awhile later when the third Jon Peters Salon opened its doors at 400 North Rodeo Drive,in Beverly Hills, things really blew up big. Right away the salon gained notice in the press as the hub of a glamorous lifestyle. Movie stars, fashion models, rock stars, and wannabes all came through our doors, bringing the hippie counterculture straight into the heart of Beverly Hills. The makeup sessions were always fun, partly due to the fact that my makeup station was right on the front corner of the salon, facing Rodeo Drive and Brighton Way, smack-dab in the center of the best people-watching in all of Beverly Hills. All I had to do was look out the window to spot stars like Jimmy Stewart, Joan Collins, Candice Bergen, Barbara Stanwyck, or Ronald Reagan passing by on their way to Jurgensen's, the popular gourmet market, or Warren Beatty and Jack Nicholson crossing the street, heading for their favorite private watering hole, the Daisy.

One afternoon Fred Astaire came gliding down Rodeo Drive as if his feet didn't even touch the pavement. That was the normal every-day traffic outside the salon. We had big windows that opened wide so that people walking by could see what we were doing. On summer days we would open the windows, and casual observers would poke their heads in to say hello or compliment whatever client I was work-ing on. Famed *Hollywood Reporter* columnist Army Archerd made it a practice to hang out on my corner, chatting through the open window while I did his wife, Selma's, makeup. He was always certain to catch sight of some famous celebrity worth mentioning in his next column. Stars like Farrah Fawcett, Ali MacGraw, Kris Kristofferson, Barbra Streisand, Ryan O'Neal, and the Supremes all crowded into the salon at one time or another. Many of them wanted me to do their eyebrows and makeup, and before long the word was out: Bobbe Joy Cosmetics was the new and innovative choice of the Hollywood in crowd and I was their go-to girl.

8

I GOT THIS!

In the end I respond to my own instincts. Sometimes they're successful and sometimes they're not. But you have to remain true to what you believe in.

—ANNA WINTOUR

On the home front my husband finally graduated law school and passed the bar exam. Rather than take a low-level position with an established law firm, he decided to be his own boss. He opened his one-man legal practice in a small unimposing office in Encino. He didn't specialize in any particular area of the law but was happy to take whatever clients walked through the door. Because he wasn't much of a go-getter, I could readily see that it was going to take a while for him to get established. That meant I would continue to be our main source of income. I was now working three days a week in Beverly Hills, two days in Encino, and one in Woodland Hills at the Jon Peters Salons. Any plans to ease off of my heavy work schedule were put on hold.

It was 1973 on a busy Saturday in the Woodland Hills salon. I was booked back to back, and, as usual, the salon was humming with the sounds of piped-in rock music and lively chatter. It was almost lunchtime, and people were calling out orders for sandwiches and salads from the nearby deli, changing their orders, making appointments, trying to pay, and driving the poor desk girl nuts. In the midst of all this lively craziness, I was intensely focused on an eyebrow cleanup, delicately tweezing one hair at a time to create the perfect natural arch for a very picky client. In the mirror I noticed a young fresh-faced girl watching me from the sidelines. Many of the salon customers liked to watch me work, but this girl was paying extra close attention. I finished and held the mirror up for my customer to see herself. Fortunately, she was completely happy with her brows. She hugged me and praised me and left a generous tip. That's when the young girl stepped forward and introduced herself.

"Hi, I'm Linda Klauss. I wish I could do what you do. I love makeup; it's my favorite thing."

I took a good look at her and sized her up the same way that Aida Grey had sized me up some five years earlier. I could see she knew how to do her makeup: her color choices were good, nothing was overdone, and her eyebrows were well shaped. She was nicely dressed, and I sensed she had a warm personality. I had been thinking for some time that I could use a personal assistant, not just as a makeup artist but someone who could work side by side with me and who could even take over some of my clients when I got overbooked. My gut instinct told me Linda would be a good candidate. On the spot I offered her a job.

"Would you like to be my assistant?"

Her eyes lit up. "Oh my God! Absolutely."

"Can you start Tuesday?"

"What time?"

My instincts about Linda were good. Her personality and work ethic meshed perfectly with mine, and it wasn't long before we became a dynamic duo. Once Linda was able to take over some of the regular makeup appointments, it allowed me to accept more clients, and pretty soon I needed additional help with the day-to-day headaches of running a thriving business.

My husband, who was still struggling to make his new law firm viable, also had a degree in accounting, and he eagerly took over handling my money. He loved running the adding machine, and the more I was able to do, the less he had to do. He was a man who liked to put his feet up. I'd come home from a hard day's work and hand over my earnings, which he eagerly took but never praised me for. On days when the take was lower than expected, he'd say things like, "Is that all you did?" It was hurtful, but I brushed it aside, unaware that little by little those comments were eating away at my self-esteem and our marriage.

If there was anything my husband enjoyed more than counting my money, it was hanging out with my salon friends like Jon, Paul, and Allen. He thought they were cool, and he relished being part of the in crowd. Our social life had started to become deeply enmeshed with my work life.

On the weekends, after salon hours, a group of us would get together for the typical California barbecues and pool parties. Several of us had young children, and we were all firmly entrenched in the middle-class version of the hippie lifestyle.

The idea of free sex had moved quickly out of the hippie culture and into the popular media, with titillating articles about new sexual norms appearing in respectable magazines like *Time* and *Newsweek*. There were lurid descriptions of "fishbowl parties," where married couples who liked to hook up with other people would put their keys in a fishbowl and whoever picked your keys out of the bowl was who you went home with. Our cool crowd shunned that kind of "low-class" behavior, and even though it was generally accepted that certain members of our select group were having extramarital affairs, for the most part we stayed out of each other's business.

Personally, I would never think of having an affair, and I trusted my husband felt the same. Admittedly, there were times when I suffered from feelings of neglect, but whatever problems we might have had, I still believed in the sanctity of marriage and worked hard to keep ours together.

• • •

Part of me found fulfillment in the kitchen, and I became known as quite a good cook. Some Saturday nights my husband would invite couples over, and after standing on my feet at work the whole day, I would cook gourmet meals for them. When I knew ahead of time that we were having guests, I would prep as much as I could the night before, and I always took great pains to set a beautiful table. Like the good little girl I was, I busted my butt to do it and do it with style.

Most of the other wives were stay-at-home moms, and part of me resented them for sitting around praising my efforts but not lifting a finger to help. On the other hand, I must admit that in some ways it made me feel special. I was the one who could do it all! I was the chef, I was the server, and I was the hostess, all while my husband sat at the head of the table like a king and said, "Bobbe, would you bring me a glass of water?" I should have poured it over his head, but that's not what good little girls do. Boy, was I stupid!

• • •

I was settling into a comfortable groove with my schedule, and Linda Klauss was working out well as my assistant, when one day an artsy-looking young man with a receding hairline walked into the Beverly Hills salon. He was a photographer named Bob Blakeman, and he asked me a question that would change my life—again.

"Can you do makeup for a photo shoot?"

My first photo shoot with Bob Blakeman was for the Broadway Department Stores, an old established chain that regularly ran ads in the *Los Angeles Times* Sunday edition. The morning of the shoot I woke up in a panic. I was a bundle of nerves. I checked and double-checked every eyebrow pencil, lipstick color, foundation, blush, mascara, face powder, eyelash curler—anything I might even remotely need—and carefully arranged everything in my black leather makeup kit. As I drove to Bob's studio through the commercial center of Beverly Hills, all I could think was, "Oh my God! I've accepted a job that I don't even know I can do." Like so many things in my life, I had jumped in feet first. Again, it was time to sink or swim.

Once I arrived at Bob's large studio in Beverly Hills, I discovered that the atmosphere was low key; everybody was going about their business with very little fuss. Bob was adjusting the lights, a young woman named Patti Altbaum was picking out clothes for the models, and an assistant was waiting to show me where I could set up. As I unpacked my kit, the feel of my clean, soft brushes, the sharpened pencils, and all the familiar tools of my trade was a calming reminder that I could do this. By the time the two models arrived, I was poised and ready to go.

This particular photo shoot was a fashion layout that Bob did pretty much every week. Patti was the stylist. It was her job to pull together the wardrobe and oversee the look of each shot.

"This top goes with those pants; this dress with these shoes . . ."

There were three or four different outfits to shoot, and Patti helped me understand that the clothes were the most important element and my job was just to make sure the models looked beautiful. The models were two attractive girls with flawless complexions who needed only the most basic makeup jobs. Making them look beautiful was a no-brainer, and I sailed through the shoot easily.

If there was ever the right job to show me that doing photo shoots wasn't anything to be afraid of, that job was it. After that first day I knew it was something that I could not only do well but also that I really enjoyed. We had fun, and as an added bonus it was the beginning of a great working relationship with Patti (which led to us becoming life-long friends) and with Bob Blakeman, who was obviously pleased with my work and hired me many more times. We became friends as well.

Little by little, as one model or hairdresser or stylist recommended me to another photographer, more photo shoots came my way. Going to different locations and working with other artists made me feel I was doing something truly creative. My schedule at the salons was still jam-packed, but I could see a time coming when photo shoots would offer me greater financial, artistic, and personal freedom. In the back of my mind I began to envision myself in this new, intriguing role, not so tied to the daily salon schedule and with more freedom to be with my family.

· · ·

Then, much to my delight, I became pregnant for a second time. Of all the roles I enjoyed, being a mother was my favorite. I took great pleasure in knowing that my son would not be an only child, that he would have the sibling I always wanted for myself when I was growing up. I embraced my second pregnancy wholeheartedly and easily integrated it into my busy schedule.

In 1971 our second child was born, a beautiful little girl we named Portia. Both my husband and I were overjoyed with this precious new baby. As much as I adored my son, there's a special kind of bond that a mother has with a little girl. A daughter is a chance to do your life over: to make her better than you are, to love her more than you were loved, and to raise her as your special gift to the world. Portia made me appreciate my own mother in a whole new way. I now understood why she had pinned so many of her hopes and dreams on me.

I quickly learned that a second child meant double the parenting work. As usual, the additional responsibility fell on my shoulders more than on my husband's. What little free time I had was now taken up with the house and the children. I was so busy I hardly noticed the subtle changes taking place in our marriage.

My husband was a man who needed lots of attention, and if he wasn't getting all of mine, he had no trouble looking elsewhere. My first clue that something was going wrong started in the bedroom. Our sex life had always been enjoyable for both of us, but suddenly he started questioning my performance, complaining that I was not multi-orgasmic. I was twenty-six years old. I had never been with another man, so admittedly my sexual experience was limited. It never occurred to me that one of the women in our circle of friends was a predatory nymphomaniac, sporting new fake boobs and screwing everybody's husband, including mine. If other people knew about it, they certainly didn't tell me.

Once he started judging me, I began to wonder whether there was somebody else involved in this relationship, because it seemed that in his mind he had held a competition and I had come out the loser. Suddenly, all my youthful insecurities came roaring back, along with a new one. I was no longer sexually attractive to my husband. Maybe I was no longer sexy to any man!

Mom, Dad, and me on the town in Las Vegas in the '50s

Dorky grade school pictures

60

My best friend, Sharon (on the left), and me at junior high school graduation

Mom with Liberace in Hawaii. My dad was playing in his orchestra.

Costume night on the cruise ship (S.S. President Cleveland) going to Yokohama, Japan. (L-R) Leslie Rosenstock, Groucho Marx as the captain, me, and the captain of the ship dressed as Groucho, 1960

My graduation picture from high school, 1962. Bouffant hairdos were all the rage. Thank goodness they eventually went out of style!

Eugenia Weston, my first hire at Bobbe Joy and present owner of Senna Cosmetics

*Handmade lashes at
Bobbe's Beauty Bar inside
Jon Peters Salon*

At my first wedding, with all my bridesmaids, July 26, 1964

Me as a happy bride with my parents, Lou and Ruth Singer

9

GOING BAD

Don't look to the approval of others
for your mental stability.

—KARL LAGERFELD

It was the night of the Christmas party at the Encino Jon Peters Salon. A group of us were in a back room behind the salon smoking pot and drinking champagne when one of the male stylists unexpectedly kissed me like I hadn't been kissed in years. Our encounter was brief—just a single kiss—but it was electric. Neither of us said anything. We slipped back into the party, and I tried my best to be a part of the jovial celebration as if nothing had happened, but I kept turning the kiss over in my mind, trying to analyze whether it had just been an impulsive act or whether there was really something there. He and I had never been attracted to each other, or at least not that I knew of. We hadn't even been particularly friendly, but that kiss changed everything.

We purposely avoided each other the rest of the night. I went home to bed, wrapped in a cocoon of tender feelings. I could have stayed there forever, except that Ian was up at the crack of dawn shouting in my ear, "Mommy, Mommy, it's time to open presents!"

Yes, even though we're Jewish, at that time we did celebrate Christmas, without the religious aspects. (That has since changed for me as I have slowly embraced my Jewish roots.) But back then I threw myself into the ritual of family and gifts, and by that evening I had come to believe that the brief kiss had been nothing more than an impetuous act, the result of too much holiday drinking and pot smoking, and that it would gradually fade away. It didn't.

The following days in the salon were a mixture of agony and ecstasy. We each tried to stay focused on our work and our clients, but we couldn't help shooting sidelong glances at one another, both keenly aware of the delicious secret we shared. Silently, we knew this powerful attraction was headed somewhere. A few days later he invited me to have lunch with him, and I accepted.

We sat in a corner booth of a neighborhood restaurant, hoping that no one would see us. We ordered lunch, and I said, "There's something I need to find out about myself." He looked at me and smiled in a sexy, comforting way, which gave me the courage to go on. "I'm having issues with my husband. He doesn't think I'm all that good in bed. Maybe there's something wrong with me. I need to know if I'm OK in the sex department." He got my drift.

A few days later he arranged for a room at the Sheraton Universal Hotel. I liked that. If I was going to have an illicit encounter, I wanted to do it in style. He gave me the room number, and my heart was racing as I knocked on the door. In my head I was saying, "What the hell am I doing here?" When he opened the door and pulled me into the room, I immediately knew why I was there.

The climactic outcome of that brief adventure completely restored my faith in my physical attraction and put me back on the road to self-worth. For a week I floated on the high from that dangerous liaison. Then, like all addictive pleasures, it made me want more.

Our "experiment" turned into an ongoing affair, a dangerous and thrilling adventure during which we continued to be colleagues and social friends and even went on a "couples trip" to Asia with our spouses.

That led to a totally insane escapade one afternoon in Bangkok when the two husbands went off to a massage parlor. My lover's wife went to take a nap, and I took a walk around a shopping mall. When I returned to my room, the phone was ringing. I answered and heard a voice say, "Meet me in room 2320." I knew immediately who it was, and it wasn't my husband. My lover had slipped out of the massage parlor for a little tryst with me, leaving my husband there, blissfully unaware of what was going on. We were young and crazy, and the peril of being caught only heightened the pleasure. It was hard to discern whether I was in love or in lust. All I knew was I was riding high on a tide that lifted everything in my life.

● ● ●

By now, I had gained a reputation as a makeup artist who could bring out a woman's natural beauty, and the business, especially at the Beverly Hills salon, was thriving. My clients now included such well-known names as Anne Bancroft and, briefly, Raquel Welch, who came to me because she wanted me to try a new look on her. Raquel was one of the most difficult clients I ever encountered. As I got to work on her, she began to tell me how she liked her makeup done, how she applied it, etc. I reminded her she'd asked for something new and different, so she suggested I try something new on one eye and keep her usual makeup on the other eye. The more I tried to help her, the more frustrated she became. She just couldn't deal with losing her old look, so she thanked me and left. Fortunately, I was in a good place with my self-esteem and didn't let it bother me. Besides, my encounter with her was only a minor annoyance. I had much more serious problems to deal with. My father, at the age of fifty-seven, had been diagnosed with colon cancer. His life expectancy was not good, two years at the most. It was a crushing blow to my mother and me and added greatly to the pressures I was under. I loved my father dearly, and the prospect of losing him was a terrible cloud hanging over my head.

• • •

I knew that my love affair was providing me with the warmth and affection that was missing in my marriage and that it was only a temporary off-ramp from an unhappy life. Like all things too good to be true, I knew this rocket to the moon would eventually come in for a hard landing.

The beginning of the end took place on a gloomy Monday when I was home from work with a head cold. I was in bed sniffling, surrounded by tissues and feeling miserable, when my husband called to inform me that he was going out for lunch.

When I asked whom he was lunching with, he said, "No one."

"Sure," I thought to myself. I knew something was up.

By this time our relationship had deteriorated to the point where I no longer believed anything he said. As soon I hung up the phone, I called one of my best friends and told her I suspected he was going to meet a woman for a nooner and that I was going out to look for him.

"Not without me," she said.

We drove down Sepulveda Boulevard, stopping at every motel to check out the parking lots. Sure enough, at the third one, there was his car. My heart stopped. I'd half hoped I was wrong, but there was no denying it; he was busted! I pulled a piece of paper out of the glove compartment of my car and wrote a note.

"Dear Ex, I hope you had a nice lunch!" I signed it "Your Wife," and I put it on the windshield of his car. I pulled my car into a spot across the street from the motel, and my friend and I hunkered down like Cagney and Lacey on a stakeout.

Suddenly, a second-floor door opened, and out he came followed by a woman wearing a wig. Despite the obvious disguise, I easily recognized her as the woman with the boob job who screwed everyone's husband. The next thing I knew, they were speeding out of the parking lot. On the return trip home, all I could think of was the conversation I knew was about to happen.

My husband admitted his guilt, and we agreed to try to patch things up, but a month later it all came to a head when he threw my anniversary present across the room and onto the bed. That, along with a few choice words, was the end of our marriage. I told him we were done. Finally, I had found my voice.

Now all I had to do was figure out how to go forward and how to tell Ian and Portia.

It was also the end of my love affair. He was eager to carry on as we had been doing for three years, but I was not. With my father dying and my impending divorce, it just wasn't in the cards.

●　●　●

No one in our family had ever been divorced, so I was a little concerned about how my parents would take it. I knew that sooner or later I would have to let them know, but I was having trouble picking up the phone to tell them. When, finally, I did call, my mother's reaction was "I'm not surprised."

"Well, I feel bad because I'm the first person in the family to get a divorce."

"You forgot," she replied. "Your grandma was divorced and remarried!"

"Right! My grandma in Petaluma who divorced her first husband and married the chicken farmer. And she had a great life!"

That gave me some comfort. When I told my father, his reaction was, "Well, it's about time."

• • •

In October 1975, my father's colon cancer progressed rapidly, and he was moved into full-time care at the Motion Picture Country Home, an amazing facility for people who worked in the film industry. I lived very close by and was on call for my father any time of day or night. He was slipping in and out of lucidity because of the heavy drugs he was on. One afternoon I got a very lively phone call from him. "Hey, Bob," he said, using his nickname for me, "you know what I'd love? A corned beef sandwich."

"I'll be right over, Dad!"

I raced to the local deli and picked up a corned beef sandwich on rye. He finished half the sandwich and washed it down with a little "2 cents plain" (seltzer water). He loved it! It was probably the last thing he truly enjoyed. Two days later he passed away.

After eleven years, my marriage was over. I left my husband, broke up with my lover, and watched as my father lost his terrible battle with cancer. Within six months the three most important men in my life were gone. I was now a divorced mother with two young children and the owner of three makeup concessions and a five-bedroom house. My entire life was in upheaval, and I was in a downward spiral that seemed like it would never end.

10

HEART TO HEART

*What lies behind us and what lies before us are
tiny matters compared to what lies within us.*

—RALPH WALDO EMERSON

Tachycardia. That's what the doctors called it. I had
experienced it off and on for years, when my heart would suddenly
start doing terrifying flip-flops and then just as suddenly it would stop
and I would be OK. It was something I had learned to live with. Shortly
after I lost the three most important men in my life, I had a major
tachycardia attack that sent me to the hospital. I was in arrhythmia
for twelve hours. The doctors were getting ready to use the paddles
on me, when, in a last-ditch effort, someone decided to try a new
drug, Inderal, that was still in the test stages. Fortunately, it worked.
My heart rhythm returned to normal, and the doctors sent me home.
Once again, the cause was listed as "unknown." By then I was aware
of the connection between my physical problems and my emotional
state of mind. I was in serious trouble, and it was time to face the one
solution I had been avoiding: psychotherapy.

In the 1970s therapy was still getting a bad rap as an indulgence for people who couldn't handle their own problems. Despite my trepidations, I knew I needed help, so I decided to give it a try.

It took some searching, but eventually I found a kind and caring therapist who helped me take an honest look at my life: my father's oppressive behavior, my parents' yelling, my husband belittling me—all the problems that instead of dealing with I had stuffed down inside of me.

In one of my therapy sessions I had a major "Aha!" moment. I was talking about my father's frightening temper: how he sometimes raged at my mom and me and how bad it made me feel. The therapist nodded knowingly and said, "That's his problem, not yours." In a flash of clarity, I understood how my "good little girl" persona had driven me to take on other people's problems as if they were my own. What a relief it was to say goodbye to that misguided little girl and lay that burden down!

For me, therapy worked, and it wasn't a protracted process that went on for years. Once I got it, I started to pull out of my deep depression. As my spirits lifted, I slowly began to believe that the world might be a safe place after all.

It was still a long eight months after my divorce before I could even think about dating. When I did, I looked at men the way men look at girls: anything for a roll in the hay. I didn't even like any of these guys. I chewed them up and spit them out. Maybe I was just trying out a new "bad girl" role, but I knew it wasn't working, and, finally, I had enough. That wasn't me, and it couldn't cure my anger or my loneliness. At night I lay alone in bed wondering whether I would ever have a meaningful relationship.

• • •

It was December 19, 1976, right around Christmas. Many of my clients and friends were concerned about me being alone on the holidays. One of them was living with a well-known photojournalist/writer, Larry Schiller, and invited me to a Christmas party at their house. I really didn't feel like going to any parties, even though I knew they would probably have a lot of interesting guests. I wanted to say no, but my entire universe of friends was encouraging me to go. When I learned that my good friend, and event-planner-extraordinaire, Randy Fuhrman was catering the party, I felt much more comfortable. I agreed to go, and Randy promised to watch over me.

I found an outfit in my closet that made me feel pretty. I put on a happy face and drove to a beautiful condo on Palm Drive in Beverly Hills. The party was in full swing when I got there. I parked myself on the sofa, and Randy sat with me for a few minutes to give me moral support. He left me to take care of business in the kitchen, and I was sitting there alone thinking, "Why am I here?" when the front door opened and in walked a girl I knew named Minah. She was with a guy who I thought was her date: the kind of guy you'd picture sitting with his dog by a roaring fire, smoking a pipe, with leather patches on the sleeves of his well-worn tweed jacket. In other words, my ideal man. The couple didn't match. Minah was very sweet, but she was known to be somewhat fast and loose, and I couldn't figure out what a guy like that would be doing with a girl who was so obviously wrong for him.

Minah and her good-looking escort made their way around the party greeting people. They finally got to me, and Minah said, "Bobbe, let me introduce you to Mitch Dawson . . . just in case you ever need a good lawyer."

"Hi, Mitch, nice to meet you." I extended my hand. He took it with a reassuring squeeze.

"Nice to meet you, Bobbe. Can I get you something to drink?"

Wow! A good-looking man who wanted to wait on me! I hadn't had that in a long time.

He returned with my drink and sat next to me. "So, Bobbe, you know my receptionist, Minah?"

Well, that was a relief. Minah was a receptionist in the law office where Mitch worked. Maybe she wasn't his date.

I nodded, "Yes."

I liked Mitch right away. We spent the remainder of the evening in deep conversation. He asked whether I'd like to have dinner with him sometime after the New Year. We were clearly interested in each other, but as I learned later, he assumed I would be busy over the holidays and he didn't want to be shot down. I was so sure that he was busy that I was a little disappointed that I would have to wait until after the first of the year. Mitch, this very handsome, sexy guy, didn't want me to forget him, so he sent a holiday card to my Rodeo Drive store, with a note: "Looking forward to seeing you soon." This gave me hope, and, sure enough, on January third the phone rang, and it was the call from Mitch I had been waiting for.

Neither of us knew what hit us. We were incredibly attracted to each other. We could hardly keep our hands off one another! We found so much to talk about that before we knew it, we were in a full-blown relationship, giving all our other dates the boot.

• • •

During that same time, I received another life-changing call, this time from Dick Zimmerman, a very well-respected photographer, telling me he'd been asked to photograph a country music singer he'd never heard of. He wanted to know whether I'd be available to do her makeup. The shoot was in Malibu, and that's about all we knew, other than the fact that it was for a record album cover.

I arrived at the appointed address in Malibu and began looking for a place to set up my kit. I found nothing but a picnic table with some benches attached—and that was it! I started to set up when a beautiful woman appeared, accompanied by three men: her husband and a couple of executives from her record company. Dick and I huddled with the executives to talk about the concept for the album cover. One side would show the artist seated on the hood of a Rolls-Royce down by the ocean's edge, while the reverse side would show her seated on the back of a pickup truck.

At that point I was introduced to my model for the shoot. Her name was Barbara Mandrell. She was a country singer, and her recording of "If Loving You Is Wrong, I Don't Want to Be Right" was rapidly climbing the charts. Personally, I'd never heard of her, though from what I gathered, she was about to become a big star. I asked her to sit on top of the table so she would be at the right height for me to work. She told me she'd never been made up by a professional before and asked if she could have a mirror so she could watch me work. I refused and told her she could change anything she wanted after I'd finished. She seemed a bit surprised by my response, but she agreed. Often, when people watch a makeup application in progress, it can look weird, so I wanted her to see it completely finished.

The makeup she was wearing was dated and didn't show off her best features, so I immediately removed it all. We began to chat, and I really liked her. She was so different from anyone I'd ever met; I was a Jewish girl from the San Fernando Valley, and she was a Southern Baptist girl originally from Oceanside, California, via Texas, now living in Tennessee. It was very helpful that my dad was in the music business. It gave us some common ground in the beginning and was the focus of most of my conversations with Barbara and her husband, Ken.

When I finally allowed her to look in the mirror, she absolutely loved the work I'd done.

The photo shoot went well, though we almost lost the Rolls-Royce because the tide came in, so we had to rush—not only to finish the shoot but also to pull the car to safety before it got swept away in the ocean! The pictures came out beautifully. Unfortunately, or perhaps fortunately, the powers that be thought the album cover was a little too Hollywood for her first major album, so they scheduled a second shoot for the cover, which we did in a studio. This time it was only a headshot, but it was a totally new take on a country music singer and very different for the times. We changed Barbara's look completely—hair, makeup, and wardrobe. We took her from a sweet country girl to a sophisticated beauty. The cover was such a success that Dick Zimmerman and I began to get calls from other country music artists asking us to create the same kind of new look for them.

At last, it seemed like both my personal life and my work were in a really good place.

● ● ●

After six months of dating, Mitch and I decided to try living together. I felt it was important to find out whether my kids and I could be comfortable with him on a day-to-day basis. We knew we were in love, and Mitch enjoyed being part of our little family, but he always had a nagging question in the back of his mind as to how the kids would accept him as a father figure. I didn't want any more children. I had undergone a surgical procedure because I had had complications with my second pregnancy. That was a hard one for Mitch, who had dreamed of having his own kids. After living together for close to a year, he moved out to do some soul-searching while I sat home feeling depressed. We were the right fit. I loved him. My kids loved him. Nothing had ever felt so right, but I knew I had to give him some time.

What kept me from slipping into a deep depression was my work. I was now affiliated with several highly respected photographers, and my client list was growing to include some top male performers like Mel Brooks, Robin Williams, and Paul Newman. One afternoon Dick Zimmerman called to ask whether I could work on a shoot for the cover of *Los Angeles* magazine. The star of the shoot was Dolly Parton. That was a no-brainer! I loved Dolly and could hardly wait to work my magic on her. On the day of the shoot Dolly arrived at Dick Zimmerman's studio ready to roll, with her hair and makeup completely done. To me her look was a little dated, and I was hoping to give her a new look that would bring out her true beauty. But I knew this was a tricky situation and I would have to tread lightly. I introduced myself. "Hi, I'm Bobbe Joy. I'm the makeup artist. I see you're all set to go, but if you need something, just let me know."

She looked me up and down—and I mean she really looked me up and down!—then she said, "Well, if I let you do something, what would you do?"

Frankly, I wanted to wipe off every lick of makeup and start all over again, but I said, "Well, I'd just clean you up a little bit." She walked away, looking pensive. Then a few minutes later she came over and said, "OK. Fix me up."

I sat her in a chair and began to clean her up and redo her makeup. At that time, I traveled with a professional makeup box filled with every requirement for any possible situation. When I finished, Dolly was so happy with what I'd done, she said, "I want one of those boxes." I thought she just wanted the makeup box. I told her I could get one for her, at which point she said, "With everything in it." Wow! That was a lot of makeup: think face makeup, pencils, brushes, eye shadow, blush, lip colors!

"And I'd like you to teach me how to do my makeup." In other words, she wanted her own personal makeup box, which I would fill with every single item I thought was right for her and only her. It was a kick—and an honor—to create something especially for Dolly Parton. Plus, she wanted me to tell her everything I knew—all my secrets!

Boy, was I excited! I still had my makeup line at the Jon Peters Salon, and I told her I'd fill up a box for her and we could meet to discuss how she should use it. She gave me her private phone number, and a week or so later, I made an appointment with her assistant and drove over to her apartment in Beverly Hills and brought "the box."

Dolly opened the door fully made up with every hair in place. I asked her how she expected me to teach her how to do her makeup when she already had all that makeup on. She immediately went into the bathroom and removed the whole lot. She even took off her wig and wrapped her own hair in a flower-petaled shower cap. Dolly was truly beautiful without a stitch of makeup on, but that was not the person either of us wanted to put out into the universe. So I began to make her up, teaching her as I went along. I went over the many colors of eye shadow, lipstick, lip gloss, and foundations I thought were right for her. I made up three or four paint-by-number charts for her so she'd be able to copy them to do her own makeup. Dolly is one of the smartest, most discerning stars I've ever worked with, and when she saw that I really knew what I was doing, she gave me her complete trust. It was the beginning of a long and wonderful relationship. And, to this day, Dolly still has those makeup charts hanging on the wall in her closet in Nashville!

• • •

Mitch and I continued to see each other, but we weren't living together. One night he invited me to attend the Emmy Awards with his clients John Astin (Gomez Addams in The Addams Family) and John's wife, Anna (a.k.a. Patty Duke, star of the TV series *The Patty Duke Show*). Anna had become my client, and I did her makeup for the Emmys. It was a real kick to be a part of the whole red-carpet scene rather than just watching it on television.

We had a great time at the Emmys, but when the limo was dropping me off at my house, I noticed that Anna was trying to get Mitch's attention; I suspected she wanted to know how things were going with us. Were we going to get married? I saw Mitch shaking his head, making it look as if things weren't going too well. I was devastated. I was ready to move forward, but obviously he wasn't.

Not long after that night, Mitch invited me to his apartment in Marina del Rey, where he'd been living since he'd left our house. It was my first time there, and I was a bit reluctant after the scene I'd witnessed on Emmy night. He greeted me warmly then excused himself, telling me to take whatever I wanted from the refrigerator. I opened the refrigerator door to get myself something to drink, and to my surprise there was nothing but a stash of wine and cheese plates and the kind of small dishes you could put out at the spur of the moment. It looked to me as if Mitch was prepared to entertain not just me but a whole string of women. My heart sank. I was already feeling pretty down that day. I had my period, I had an eye infection, and I felt very much under the weather.

Then Mitch walked slowly down the stairs and came to stand next to me.

"You know, your birthday is November sixth, and my birthday is November eighth. Why don't we do something special on the seventh?"

"Oh, OK," I mumbled. "Like what?

"Why don't we get married?"

Yes, just like that. After a few months apart, Mitch had concluded that he didn't want to live without me, and that was exactly the way I felt about him.

On a crisp, clear Tuesday, November 7, 1978, we were married at a beautiful restaurant in Beverly Hills, surrounded by friends and family. Among the guests were Linda Klauss, Allen Edwards, Randy Fuhrman, my school friend Sharon, actress Mariette Hartley and her husband, my kids and my mother, and Mitch's parents and brothers. John Astin was our best man. I wore a beautiful lavender chiffon dress from a French shop on Rodeo Drive, and I did my own hair and makeup. I felt beautiful, sexy, and filled with gratitude. It was one of the happiest days of my life.

We honeymooned in Acapulco and started our marriage in the duplex I had rented in Beverly Hills. In Mitch I had finally found the partner every woman dreams of: a man who was solid and strong and gave me the love and respect I needed to thrive.

Mitch and me at our wedding on November 7, 1978

One of my mom's beautiful hand-painted porcelain pieces. She called this one "Strawberries and Cream," 1977

Happily ever after with Portia and Ian

Mitch, Anna (Patty Duke), and me

Anna (Patty Duke) and me
celebrating a holiday in the
kitchen, of course

The principal cast of It Takes Two. I did the
makeup for Helen Hunt, Patty Duke, and Billie
Bird. Even Richard Crenna once! 1988

Barbara Mandrell as a snow queen for her fan club calendar, 1989

Barbara Mandrell in a bunny costume for her fan calendar, 1989, doing her makeup

Dolly Parton, cover of Playboy, 1978 (courtesy of Mario Casilli Photography)

11

A FULL-TIME JOB

Fashion changes, style endures.

—COCO CHANEL

The kids settled in, I settled in, and Mitch easily accepted his role as stepfather: coaching Ian's Little League and soccer teams; driving my daughter, Portia, to dance classes; and sometimes doing carpool runs. We worked hard at becoming a family. My former husband hung around at the beginning, but then he began to default on his financial responsibilities. We went through many court appearances to retrieve the back child support due, and even though the judges would tell him to pay up, he continued to fall behind, citing "lack of funds." He owned two Mercedes and a beautifully furnished home and traveled all over the world. No wonder he was pleading lack of funds! Then, out of the blue, he came up with another option. His attorney called Mitch to ask whether he would like to adopt Ian and Portia. All we had to do was forfeit the money he owed for child support. The kids were now thirteen and seventeen. They had been spending very little time with their biological father over the past couple of years. So that very night we took them out for a meal and told them of their dad's proposal. The response was immediate: "Yes! And can we change our last name?"

One year later the adoption was final, and they were able to start college and high school with their new last name.

• • •

I had a new name too. I was now Bobbe Dawson. (I actually didn't use the name Dawson professionally until later, when I started using it in relation to my community activities, where I was known as Bobbe Joy Dawson.)

Everything was going well, and my career was on a roll. Photo shoots were becoming a full-time job, and I could see my life moving in a whole new direction. Things were changing at the salon, too. Jon and Lesley Ann Warren had divorced in 1974, and Jon had been in a serious relationship with Barbra Streisand for over two years. She would come into the salon on a regular basis, and we became friendly enough that I was invited out to her house in Malibu's Ramirez Canyon. This particular home was a true reflection of the times. There was a round bed-like couch in the living room with lots and lots of pillows, and the whole place was like an upscale hippie pad. On the outside, Barbra was shy and somewhat off-putting, but her home was a warm and friendly place that reflected her true personality.

Like most people I was in awe of her amazing talent, not just because I was a fan but because my dad thought so highly of her. He had recorded with her and said she used her voice like a musical instrument, and he admired how incredibly professional she was. Like him, she was a total perfectionist.

Watching Jon and Barbra one afternoon, I could see how smitten he was by this amazing woman. Sparked by his infatuation with someone who was even more accomplished than he, Jon was already seeing a bigger, more creative outlet for his talents. As their relationship evolved, I could see Jon becoming less and less interested in the salon and more and more interested in Barbra's world of Hollywood and the movies.

Jon's first entry into the movie business was as a producer of the film *A Star Is Born*, which starred Barbra and Kris Kristofferson. For the premiere of the film I was hired to do glamour makeup for singer Rita Coolidge, who was then Kris Kristofferson's wife. Rita also asked my assistant, Linda, to make up their daughter. When it was time to pay, Rita pulled out a brown paper bag filled with hundred-dollar bills. No purse—just a paper bag! They walked out of the salon looking beautiful, and Linda and I were left with our hands full of cash and our mouths hanging open.

A Star Is Born was a huge hit, and in 1978 Jon left the hairdressing business to focus on his nascent film-producing career. With Jon gone, the salon didn't have quite the same joie de vivre. By now, my photo shoot work was going really well, and I decided the time had finally come to give up the salon makeup business and pursue a career as a freelance makeup artist. It wasn't that difficult a decision. The freelance world offered all the advantages I wanted: more money, less work, and more time to spend with Mitch and the children. I bit the bullet and closed up shop, leaving a lot of unhappy clients, some of whom I continued to work with privately.

• • •

Dick Zimmerman, the photographer I had worked with on Barbara Mandrell's album cover, became one of the most in-demand photographers for high-profile celebrities and began hiring me regularly as his go-to makeup artist. It was a kick to spend the day putting makeup on stars like Priscilla Presley, Robin Williams, Stockard Channing, and Jane Seymour. We created new looks for many of them, and, of course, I was learning from them, too. Stockard was the first person to show me the trick of using a certain kind of tape and some clips to achieve an instant—although temporary—face-lift. (More about that later.)

The album cover we did for Barbara Mandrell received so much acclaim that she began to call me for other assignments: award shows, television appearances, PR, commercials, and more album covers. Shortly after she won the 1980 Best Female Vocalist at the Country Music Awards in Nashville, she hired me as her personal makeup artist. In fact, I was with her for most of the awards she received over the years. She'd fly me to Nashville and put me up in her house, where I saw firsthand that Southerners are truly the most hospitable people in the world. Staying at Barbara's house was like staying with family. She never stopped trying to feed me and loved to sit and chat.

Being backstage with Barbara at the Grand Ole Opry and watching the celebrities go in and out of their dressing rooms was one of my favorite things to do. There were never enough dressing rooms, so we often had to share with other artists, which gave me the opportunity to meet some of the most famous stars in the country music world, including Tammy Wynette, who became another one of my country music clients. The first time hairdresser Rahn McDow and I worked with Tammy, we persuaded her to change her old-fashioned style for something new, hip, and modern. She loved it. We all loved it, and it made her look so much younger and prettier.

As a result of the work Dick Zimmerman and I were doing together, both our reputations began taking on a life of their own. Dick and I realized that we were having a transformative effect on the look of country music artists, and we decided to really run with it. We knew how to make these artists look fabulous, and they all wanted that.

In fact, Barbara Mandrell always used to say to me, "Do my makeup like I'm a fashion model." She had the most beautiful eyes, and she loved it when I would go wild with very high-fashion looks for her. The word began to get around, not only in the country music circles but also in the broader celebrity world, that Bobbe Joy was changing the look of glamour makeup. Pretty soon everyone wanted to know *what* I was doing and how I was doing it.

Around that time, I was contacted by Jan Glenn and Don Nelson, the co-hosts of *Good Morning Houston*, which was a popular show back in the day. They had read about me mainly because of how we were changing the faces of the country music stars. The viewers in Texas were enamored with all that kind of glamour, and so they wanted to know who did the makeup. The show created a segment where I would do an on-camera makeover on a woman they selected. I was always introduced as the "Hollywood makeup artist to the stars." I brought Linda with me and my hairdresser friend Ron. They flew us in every few months, and we would stay at Houston's Warwick Post Oak Hotel, which had a beauty salon. We would do the show, and then people could make appointments to come in and get their makeup done.

We shot the segment at the studio and then went to the salon, where we would shoot the makeover. I remember that every time we would come to town, there were always two or three typically pretty Texas big-hair blondes, along with a variety of people, younger women, older women. The segment was so popular that I remember going to the mall and being recognized. I thought that was really funny since I'm always behind the scenes doing the celebrities.

My time in Texas was a lot of fun, and doing my work, and explaining it as I went along, was a real on-camera learning experience. Eventually, it became easier and easier for me to do that. Before I knew it, I was making appearances on all kinds of shows, teaching people about makeup, and talking about the importance of keeping yourself looking good. I truly enjoyed sharing my philosophy about what makeup can do for a woman and how important it is to your overall sense of well-being.

●　●　●

Barbara Mandrell and Dolly Parton were now regular clients, and their careers were soaring. Both of them wanted to work exclusively with me whenever possible. We had become very close, and our relationships had moved beyond the professional into real friendships.

The only sour note occurred when Dick Zimmerman became upset because Barbara Mandrell wanted me to come to Nashville. It was as if he thought I should only be working for him and I shouldn't be allowed to take other jobs. I was already working with other photographers, but Dick thought that going off with Barbara was a violation of his understanding that I was his personal makeup artist. Sadly, we parted ways. I hated to lose my close friendship with Dick, because we worked so well together, had done so many memorable shoots, and had made a lasting impact on the beauty world. I was grateful for all the work and exposure he had given me and always would be indebted to him.

Fortunately, my horizons continued to expand, and I could now proudly list some of the finest photographers on the West Coast on my résumé. One of my all-time favorites was Harry Langdon Jr. Harry was the son of the famed silent movie comedy star Harry Langdon Sr. The younger Harry was known as the king of glamour photos.

When I first met him, I was intimidated. It was *Harry Langdon*, and I didn't get that warm and fuzzy feeling right away. He was very businesslike and extremely professional in a lot of ways, and he had a clear picture of what he was doing and didn't waste time. So you were never at a photo shoot for an entire day with Harry. He worked quickly and could get the shot in a finite amount of time, and that was it. One of the things Harry was really good at was retouching. Today, if I were to ask him, he probably wouldn't retouch anymore because you can do it digitally, but that's why his work looked so pretty back then. A shoot with Harry Jr. always pushed me beyond my limits. Harry was a perfectionist, and he expected everyone around him to perform to his high standards. He had the reputation that he could capture anyone's true beauty, as he did in his glamorous photos of Barbara Mandrell.

Harry was such a consummate artist. Being around him, I constantly learned new things, like how to work with lighting and photo backgrounds. It was an education I could not have gotten anywhere else.

Often, I was pushed to go out of my comfort zone and create a completely new look for an actress or celebrity. Could I manage a photo shoot in which I was asked to glue flowers and rhinestones on women's faces?! Absolutely! If I didn't know how to do something, I quickly learned it. I thrived on the challenge and the excitement of doing something new and creative.

My other great teacher was photographer Dick Broun—known as just Broun—an extremely creative artist whose visual approach leaned toward fine art. Shari Belafonte was one of the actresses we worked with, and Dick encouraged me to experiment with different looks. We photographed her with her face surrounded in fur, which made her exquisite features pop. Shari was, and still is, a great beauty, and she was the perfect model for my work. I recently sent her that same picture, and she wrote back to say that that particular shot was one of her all-time favorites.

A character shot that Dick took of my husband, Mitch, was the best photo ever taken of him.

Matthew Rolston!? Oh my God, talk about being artistic and talented! I worked with him for the cover shot of Patty Duke's book *Call Me Anna*. His background was art. It wasn't just going to photography school—it was art. These guys were more than photographers. They understood lighting, which, of course, you have to know as a photographer. But they really honestly understood makeup. They understood how to light somebody to get the most out of makeup, how color and backdrops and texture could work together to make the eyes pop or even out a skin tone. That was what was most exciting to me, the art of it all, the whole fabulous photograph that my work was a significant part of.

Over the years there were many other outstanding photographers I had the pleasure of working with. On one occasion Dolly Parton flew me to New York for two days of photo shoots. The first was with Patrick Demarchelier, a brilliant French fashion photographer, and the following day we did a shoot with Tim White, another great photographer of celebrities and models.

Way back when, I did a shoot on a beach in Malibu that promised to be exciting because for the first time I would be working with a female photographer, a young woman by the name of Annie Leibovitz. It was so long ago that I have no recollection of what we shot, but I love to boast that I had the honor of doing a photo shoot with this now-iconic photographer—literally before anyone knew her.

From all these amazing artists I learned the basic principles of artistic photography: how even the slightest shift in angles or camera position can completely change the mood and look of a shot, how a light positioned low appears to distort the features, and how a higher light can result in more prominent cheekbones or, if used badly, can elongate nose shadows. It was a delicate art of tweaking, moving, adjusting, and positioning to achieve exactly the right look, and I was proud that my contribution played an important role in the success of the final product. I was having such a good time I never thought about how demanding the work was or the toll it was taking on my body. I was doing my dream job and loving every minute of it.

12

THE TRUE COST
OF FAME

*A respectable appearance is sufficient to make
people more interested in your soul.*

—KARL LAGERFELD

As a result of my previous work with Dolly Parton, photographer
Mario Casilli hired me to do her makeup for a *Playboy* magazine
photo spread. Mario did a lot of work for *Playboy,* and his centerfold
nudes were always the highlight of the magazine. It surprised me that
Dolly would agree to appear in *Playboy,* but as Mario explained, this
assignment was going to be different. Dolly would agree to do the shoot
only if she could keep her clothes on. She didn't mind appearing in
the magazine looking sexy, but posing nude went against her religious
beliefs. Fortunately for Dolly she was a big enough star that she could
name her own terms. To their credit, the *Playboy* editor and art director
put their heads together and came up with a clever concept.

Dolly appeared on the cover wearing a Playboy bunny outfit complete with bunny ears, and on the inside photo spread she
posed with a man in a full-size white rabbit suit. It was an amusing

and tasteful layout, and her cover shot became an iconic image for *Playboy. Playboy's* faithful readers may have been disappointed not to see Dolly in the buff, but no one could deny that she was an enticing package even with her clothes on.

By then, I was doing Dolly's makeup for all kinds of occasions, just as with Barbara Mandrell: award shows, photo shoots, album covers, and television appearances. It was always fun and interesting to be around Dolly because she was, and is, one of the smartest women I've ever known. Her songwriting and singing are inspirational, and the way she shares her personal experience of growing up "poor but happy" makes fans instantly relate to her and love her. Plus, Dolly has another quality that I greatly admire: she is loyal to the bone.

When she had her own television show, Dolly was unhappy with the makeup artist hired by the production company, so she asked me to come do her makeup. I wasn't in the union, so I had to hide in the dressing room and do her makeup on the sly. It was nerve-wracking, and I didn't want Dolly to get into trouble, so I did only one show. Not long after, I received a beautiful handwritten card from Dolly telling me how much she appreciated the work I'd done. She knew the producers were concerned that our subterfuge would get them in trouble with the union, but she didn't want it to end without expressing her appreciation for what I did.

• • •

I did get my shot at television soon after, with Barbara Mandrell, who had become so popular she was now starring in her very own TV show, *Barbara Mandrell and the Mandrell Sisters.* Alongside her were her two very talented sisters, Louise and Irlene. Even though I still wasn't in the union, Barbara insisted I be the personal makeup artist for her and her sisters. This time the producers accommodated me and hired an additional union makeup artist who would take care of the singers, dancers, and guest stars while I stayed far away from the set in an upstairs dressing room to work on the three Mandrell sisters.

The show rehearsed Monday to Thursday and taped on Thursday and Friday nights, so Barbara, her sisters, and the entire family had to relocate from Nashville to Los Angeles on a temporary basis. My husband, Mitch, was instrumental in helping them rent a house in Beverly Hills that we thought Barbara would appreciate for its privacy and luxury. It didn't quite work out that way. In the South the homes are far apart with lots of space in between, not shoulder to shoulder the way they are in Beverly Hills. Barbara said, "I could hear that guy blowing his nose next door." It didn't matter that it was on Rodeo Drive in the swankiest area of Beverly Hills; if she could hear her neighbor sneeze, it wasn't her idea of a great place to live.

I think Barbara read the tea leaves about Los Angeles. It was a den of vipers that just didn't appeal to her, and she never quite got comfortable here. One of the things that was hardest for her was the feeling that she always had to be "on," that she was a personality and that she had to live up to that.

Only in the quiet times when she was with friends could she let her hair down. Occasionally, Mitch and I would go out to dinner with Barbara and her husband, Ken, but she was so busy working on the television show when she was out here that she barely had time to breathe. The quiet times were hard to come by.

The TV show was a killer. I think it took courage on her part to have to open up and realize that if she was going to be a star, she would have to do some things that didn't sit well with her Christian values. That didn't mean she had to sleep with anybody but her husband, but she had to learn to dance, and, suddenly, she's being tossed around, with gay guys grabbing her crotch. It was quite a departure. She was fortunate to have a great choreographer, Scott Salmon, and the best dance partner ever, Vince Paterson, who went on to choreograph all the great Michael Jackson and Madonna videos. Barbara knew she didn't want to be some ordinary person being flipped around. She wanted to know what she was doing. With Scott's and Vince's help, she and her sisters all learned to be good dancers.

Every week the sisters had to learn new music, a new dance number, and various comedy sketches. There were solos and instrumental numbers; Barbara played a gazillion different instruments. Her sister Irlene played drums, and Louise played several instruments, but neither came close to the number of instruments Barbara played. Every show featured multiple costume changes, and thanks to the brilliant award-winning designer Bill Hargate, the costumes were creative and colorful and made people sit up and take notice. But every costume change required some adjustment to the makeup, and sometimes it was drastic, especially when it involved some kind of wacky character.

Working on the show was where I really learned how to think on my feet; for instance, if I didn't have a color I needed, I had to create it, which is how I became so good at mixing makeup, a skill that would serve me well later in life. But this was an aspect of show business that was all very new to me. My job had always been to make women look pretty; now I was being asked to make them up as characters for sketches. That was eye opening and daunting.

The Mandrell sisters enjoyed getting ready for the show together and didn't want to be in separate dressing rooms, so they all shared one gigantic room. Hair was done in the dressing room, but the bathroom was where I worked. It was just about large enough to house a sink and a toilet. Anyone wanting to talk to the sisters while they were being made up would have to sit on the toilet! Quite a few famous names wound up perched on that toilet, one of whom was Phyllis Diller. They did a skit in which Barbara dressed to look like Phyllis and pretended to be her, so Phyllis came and sat on the toilet so I could copy her makeup! She thought that was pretty funny and let loose with one of her signature raucous laughs, which made us all crack up. It isn't easy to do makeup when you're laughing your head off, but being around Phyllis, you couldn't help but have a good time. She sure knew how to lighten the mood! That was so much fun!

Another time Barbara had to be made up to look like Grand Ole Opry star Minnie Pearl; there was no one as lovely as Minnie, one of the nicest people I've ever met, and very smart, though making Barbara up to look like Minnie was quite a feat.

Dolly Parton was also a guest star on the show, and for one skit I had to make Barbara up to look like Dolly. Since I'd made Dolly up so many times, this was no big challenge. Barbara was outfitted with ginormous boobs. She came onstage pretending to be Dolly, and Dolly snuck onto the stage behind her, mocking Barbara's imitation. Then Dolly eyed her boobs and said, "What'ya got in there? Your two sisters?" It was that kind of fun show.

Because we taped on Friday night, I would work seventeen hours straight on Fridays. As difficult as this was for me—and it was an enormous amount of work—it was more difficult for the sisters, especially Barbara. She would stay up until all hours rewriting her introductions so they sounded more like her rather than the hired writers. She had to deal with dance rehearsals and singing rehearsals and worked on the comedy routines, never getting enough sleep or enough to eat. During her breaks she couldn't talk at all, in order to save her voice. She was constantly exhausted. I felt so bad for her—and for all the girls— because they were so overworked. And people think that showbiz is all glitz and glamour!

One of the best parts of working on the show was all the celebrities I met, some of the biggest stars of the day, like Kenny Rogers, Debbie Reynolds, Roy Rogers and Dale Evans, Paul Anka, Glen Campbell, Andy Gibb, Gladys Knight and the Pips, Bob Hope, Brenda Lee, Donny Osmond, Tony Orlando, Paul Williams, Johnny Cash, Ray Charles, Tom Jones, the Smothers Brothers, Danny Thomas, and Andy Williams. What a privilege it was to see these great artists at work!

• • •

Another great country star I was fortunate to spend quite a lot of time with was Tammy Wynette, one of the loveliest and most troubled people I met in country music. Like Barbara Mandrell and Dolly Parton, Tammy was close to my age. We were all in our early thirties, and it was if we were all girlfriends.

I worked with Tammy on photo shoots and television shows and also had the opportunity to work with her in Las Vegas. Whenever we worked in Nashville, I'd stay in her home, and she couldn't have been more hospitable, including cooking breakfast for me!

I spent a lot of time hanging out with Tammy, and early on I learned that she was living with a lot of physical pain; she'd had several abdominal surgeries that had caused internal scarring. She even had surgeries to repair former surgeries. The pain was very debilitating, and she pretty much lived on pain medication.

I remember two occasions when I was privy to some really disturbing and sad situations with Tammy. I was in Nashville, doing her makeup for a show at the Grand Ole Opry. We were in her bathroom; she was seated on a stool, and I was facing her. As I worked on her makeup, I realized she was having trouble comprehending what was going on around her. I was trying to keep her engaged in conversation, but I could see she was having a problem focusing. Before I knew it, she slid off the chair, and I leapt over to grab her before she hit the floor. It was very scary, but then she seemed to rally. I finished her makeup, and she did the show, but to this day I'll never know how she got through it.

Over time, she would ask for more and more pain medication. She needed to have a port inserted into her chest in which to inject the medication so that the doctors didn't have to keep injecting it into her veins. Tammy became hopelessly addicted, but it was clear that she was in agony and couldn't function without the drugs.

The most frightening experience occurred at NBC Studios in Burbank. Tammy was preparing for the *Tonight Show* with Jay Leno. In the dressing room, I literally had to hold my hand up to her forehead to stop it from drooping while I did her makeup. All she wanted to do was close her eyes, and, obviously, I couldn't work that way. She kept crying for more medication to ease her pain. Her husband, Ritchie, finally gave in to her pleas, and it became obvious that, after flying all the way to Los Angeles and putting in all the rehearsal work, there was no way she could go onstage.

I believe this was the beginning of the end for Tammy. She could no longer pull it together and go to work. I'd never experienced anything like this in my career, and it made me incredibly sad because I really loved her. She had a beautiful voice and a beautiful soul. When she died at age fifty-five of a blood clot, it was a terrible loss not only to her friends but also to the whole country music world.

*Barbara Mandrell portrait
(courtesy of Dick Zimmerman)*

*Back row: Barbara Mandrell and her
sister Louise; bottom row: her mother,
Mary, and her youngest sister, Irlene*

Barbara and me in Las Vegas

Dolly and me at the Academy Awards

My dad, Lou "Label" Singer, at a recording session with Sammy Davis Jr. in the '60s. They were pals.

Beautiful photo of Tammy Wynette (courtesy of Harry Langdon Jr.)

Autographed photo of Tammy Wynette (courtesy of Harry Langdon Jr.)

Dolly Parton, Barbara Mandrell, and me on set

Patty Duke autobiography book cover, 1987 (courtesy of Matthew Rolston)

Dolly Parton book cover, 1994 (courtesy of Patrick Demarchelier)

Anna (Patty Duke) and her husband, Mike Pearce, and me

13

A MOTHER'S WORST FEAR

*Out of suffering have emerged the strongest souls;
the most massive characters are seared with scars.*

—KAHLIL GIBRAN

In 1978 (long before Mitch and I were married), I sold my big house in Woodland Hills, where I had lived with my first husband and the kids, and I moved to a duplex in Beverly Hills. Ian was eleven years old and Portia was seven, and at that time the majority of my work was in the Beverly Hills salon, so the move made a lot of sense. Added to that was the great reputation of the Beverly Hills school district, which made the move even more attractive. Nevertheless, moving out of the Valley to another part of the city brought with it some insecurities and self-doubt. Despite its worldwide renown, Beverly Hills is really a small town. Many of my new neighbors had been born and raised in Beverly Hills, had gone to school there, and were well integrated into the community. I, on the other hand, was an outsider, a Valley girl, entering their neck of the woods and trying to make a life in a place where outsiders weren't always welcome. Sure, people were nice enough, but they didn't necessarily embrace me with open arms.

After Mitch and I got married, we realized that even though we both worked in Beverly Hills, neither of us had close friends there, so we slowly got involved in community activities. I enrolled Portia in the Brownies, joined several local organizations, and eventually went on to serve on the Board of Directors of the Beverly Hills Chamber of Commerce. Mitch was equally, if not more, involved than I in community affairs. As a lawyer his skills were invaluable, leading him to serve on many boards. He became president of both the Century City and the Beverly Hills Rotary Clubs and chairman of the planning commission for the city. Each and every one of these volunteer organizations brought us closer to the people who lived and worked in Beverly Hills and made us feel a part of the community.

The children had no problem fitting in. Both of them were smart and good looking, had great personalities, and easily made new friends. Forgive me for sounding like a proud mother, but I must admit I have very beautiful children. When they were younger, people would stop me in the street to comment on their looks. Ian, my first born, had a thick head of curls that I left long, because in 1967 hippie styles were in full bloom. I dressed him in black T-shirts, jeans, suede fringed vests, and puka shell necklaces. People would exclaim, "She's so beautiful," and Ian would yell, "I'm a boy!" so eventually I cut his hair and dressed him a bit less elaborately.

My daughter, Portia, became more beautiful as she matured. By the time she was twelve, she had already done a bit of modeling. A photographer friend named Zhivago said he'd love to take pictures of her, so Mitch and I discussed it. I knew Zhivago quite well; at one time he'd been dating my friend Patti, the wardrobe stylist. Even at twelve, I could see that Portia had the potential to be a model or an actress. She was slender and had flawless skin and great bone structure. She was already expressing interest in a modeling or acting career, so Mitch and I decided to let her do the photo shoot.

Zhivago's studio was one large, open room. In one corner a flimsy partition had been set up to create a cubicle used as a dressing room. I had brought several outfits for Portia so she could do a couple of different looks. The wardrobe was sophisticated fashion clothing, much like what Brooke Shields was doing at the time. Zhivago had set up the lights and backdrop with the help of a young assistant while his girlfriend spent most of the shoot sitting in a corner watching the photo shoot. The shoot went well. Portia was very relaxed about the whole thing and performed like a pro. We finished, and Portia and I went back to the cubicle. While I was helping her change into her street clothes, I could hear the girlfriend on the other side of the cubicle, talking on the phone. As I gathered up our things, I was startled by a sharp crack like a car backfiring. I flinched from the sound, and before I knew it, Portia was crumbling to the floor, crying, "Mommy, Mommy, Mommy!" I grabbed for her and saw blood oozing from her denim jacket. Immediately, I realized that Portia had been shot.

What we didn't know was that Zhivago's studio had been broken into several times, so he kept a gun in his oversized pants. When the photo shoot was finished, he took the gun from his pants and placed it on the small table next to his girlfriend. While she chatted on the phone, she picked up the gun and absentmindedly began playing with it like it was a toy. Bang! The 22-caliber bullet pierced the flimsy partition and entered Portia's shoulder.

Complete panic ensued. The girl who shot Portia was hysterical. Everyone started running around in circles. No one knew quite what to do. So they did nothing. I was the first one to get my wits together, and I grabbed the phone and dialed 911. An operator assured me an ambulance would arrive in minutes. It felt like forever. Portia couldn't feel her legs, and already I was fearing the worst—a spinal injury could mean complete paralysis. While waiting for the ambulance, I called Mitch at his gym.

"Portia's been shot!" I yelled.

"Yeah, I know. You're at the photo shoot, right?"

"No! She's been shot with a GUN! Meet me at Cedars's emergency!"

Finally, the ambulance arrived. The EMTs were prepared to take her to a small local hospital. I rebelled—Cedars-Sinai or nothing! That's where all our doctors were, and I would take nothing less. Fortunately, I had some Valium in my purse and was able to take one once we got into the ambulance. It calmed me down a little. Mitch was waiting for us at the hospital, and we watched as they wheeled Portia on a gurney into the emergency examining room. Little did we know that her lung had collapsed and the doctors had to insert a chest tube to re-inflate her lungs—without anesthesia. The worst part was not knowing the extent of her injuries. The time in the waiting room seemed like hours. Repeatedly, I asked the nurse on duty if she had any new information. Finally, the doctor appeared and gave us the word.

"We took X-rays, and there's not going to be any long-term issues in terms of paralysis."

Mitch and I held onto each other and gave a sigh of relief.

"The bullet bounced around inside her and lodged itself next to her third vertebra, causing spinal shock, but it hasn't done damage to her spine. She's one lucky girl."

Despite the good news, we were still scared. How was this going to affect Portia? Not just physically but how was this going to affect her emotionally? There was no way the doctors could tell us that.

After a few days the feeling began to come back to Portia's lower extremities. She spent a few more days recuperating in the hospital before she was able to come home. The whole ordeal was beyond terrifying. For the longest time I feared what the actual residual effects were going to be, and I felt completely and utterly helpless. I felt like it was all my fault. What did I do? I'd brought her there, and I'd made her do this photo session—how stupid of me to do that. As hard as I had worked to get over my self-blame issues, this time I didn't have anyone else to blame. I knew those emotional scars would remain with me. What I will never know is how it truly affected Portia.

The truth is it really was just a stupid accident. The girl who shot Portia disappeared. She had no money; she was just a child. Zhivago had no money whatsoever. Eventually, Portia was able to collect something for all her pain and suffering from an insurance policy the owner of the studio had. But it was certainly not a life-changing amount.

Portia and I both went into therapy, but neither of us got much out of it. It was such a trauma that the most we could learn to do was live with it. I didn't want to tip-toe around Portia, but now here I was, just like my mother, scared about a lot of the stuff she wanted to do. Some of it was truly risky, like waterskiing and motorcycle riding. I saw danger at every turn, until I finally had to come to the realization that those were things that I had no control over anymore.

As for Portia, the bullet ended up lodging so close to her spine that the doctors felt it would do more harm than good to remove it. I don't know to what degree Portia has learned to live with the trauma of that terrible day, but there was an interesting follow-up to the whole story.

One day Portia was in a store when a girl she didn't recognize came up to her and said, "I want to give you this," and handed her a package, something that she had bought at the store. "I want to give you this, and I want to tell you who I am, and I want to tell you how I've suffered and how terrible I feel. I'm not asking you to forgive me. I just want you to know how sorry I am."

That night when Portia called me, I could hear the flood of painful memories in her voice as she described the encounter and her reaction.

"Number one, I don't want what she gave me, but, number two, I told her 'It's over. It's long done.' I just couldn't give her the 'I forgive you' or whatever she wanted. I don't need her to be my friend. If it made her feel better, fine . . ."

Knowing Portia, she might have added, ". . . and I hope you learned from it."

We all learned from it, but I'm not exactly sure what it was we learned. To this day I hear her twelve-year-old voice crying out, "Mommy, Mommy, Mommy," and I still relive the terror of that awful moment.

14

DOWN-HOME COUNTRY GIRL

Be the change that you wish to see in the world.

—MAHATMA GANDHI

What are the odds that a nonreligious Jewish girl from the San Fernando Valley in L.A. and a devout Christian Southern girl from Nashville would become lifelong friends? Whatever the odds, Barbara Mandrell and I defied them. You know that one friend whom you can call even though you haven't seen her in a year and when she picks up the phone it's like no time has passed? That's Barbara and me. Over the twenty years we worked together, we embraced each other's families, our children played together, our husbands became friends, we went skiing together, and we did all those activities, beyond the daily work routine, that create a bond of friendship that lasts a lifetime.

Barbara is a true Southern girl, born in Houston, Texas. Barbara's enormous musical talent was recognized early on when she was performing in a family band. In 1960 at the tender age of eleven she was discovered by country bandleader Joe Maphis. She became a featured act, playing steel guitar, and she toured with Maphis, Johnny Cash, and Patsy Cline. By the time she was twenty, she was a seasoned performer. When stardom came her way, she was ready for it.

It was my good fortune to meet Barbara just when her career was about to take off, on that fateful day in Malibu at the Rolls-Royce album cover shoot. I like to think that we came together through some kind of cosmic intervention, because it was the beginning of a brand-new phase for both of us. I was there to help Barbara make the transition from a talented country music artist into an international star by changing her look from "country" to "glamour." In turn my association with her provided me with an entrée into an exciting world that very few people ever get to experience.

Our close friendship grew out of the fact that I was always extremely honest with Barbara, and for her, that was a good thing, because there were a lot of people who were bs-ing her through the years. I think she knew I wouldn't do that. From time to time, she would ask me about different career-related problems or personal situations, and I would give my honest opinion. It wasn't always taken, but I would definitely give my opinion. So even though there was a business relationship, there was also a girlfriend relationship. If she was here right now, she would probably be washing the dishes in the kitchen. One time she stayed at my house, when I got up in the morning, what she was doing? Washing the dishes. That's just who she is. I think it's part of her wanting to stay grounded. She was well aware that the higher you climb, the harder it is to stay in touch with who you really are, so she cherished those moments when she could just be her true down-home self.

Barbara was nominated or asked to perform at pretty much every award show, and I was always there at her side. One of my all-time favorites was the Country Music Awards, where everyone who was anyone in the music world mixed and mingled. Every genre, from country to rock, they were all there, up for awards, presenting, or performing. Everybody hung out in the dressing rooms, which were very large with long makeup tables on each side of the room, with all the stars lined up doing their makeup or having it done. I remember when the Judds were on the bill. The youngest daughter, Ashley, who later became a wonderful actress, would sit on the floor of the dressing room and watch me do makeup. Obviously, she was already thinking about her future.

At the American Music Awards, I was hanging out in the green-room, which is where all of us who worked with the celebrities would go while the celebs were working. The room was mobbed, and I was looking for somewhere to sit, when from across the room I heard someone shout, "Hey, Mama!" I turned to recognize a welcoming smile and instantly flashed back to when my son, Ian, was fifteen years old and was working at Abercrombie and Fitch in the Beverly Center. One day Ian told me he had met this lovely guy who worked at another cool men's store called GHQ. Ian wanted us to meet him, so Mitch and I went there thinking that Ian just wanted us to buy him some clothes. We met his friend, a nice-looking young man with fabulous blue eyes. Not long after, Ian invited him to our home for dinner. While we were at the table, the young man said, "I'm going to be a rock star." Mitch and I looked at each other thinking, "Sure, right!" Then he announced, "My name is going to be Romeo Blue." Well, that made sense with those beautiful blue eyes.

The young rock wannabe started inviting Portia and Ian to the Herb Alpert Studios, where he was laying down music tracks he had written. As it turned out, he did become a rock star, but not before Romeo Blue and his blue contact lenses were replaced with his own soulful brown eyes and given name: Lenny Kravitz. Lenny, Ian, and Portia had remained close friends. Now here I was many years later at the American Music Awards, looking for a place to sit, when I heard that shout from across the room and turned to see Lenny grinning at me and pointing to his lap, inviting me to have a seat. His young dream had come true, and now he was Lenny Kravitz, superstar! It was a thrill to see him.

• • •

For many years Rahn McDow was the hairstylist for Barbara and her sisters. One time Rahn and I were in Washington, DC, to do Barbara's hair and makeup when she was performing for President George H.W. Bush. Like everyone else attending the event, we had to pass through the Secret Service and their drug-sniffing dogs. We were all milling around in the foyer, waiting for the doors to open, and the Secret Service was everywhere. President and Mrs. Bush were about ten feet away from us, talking to Barbara. We'd prepped her hair and makeup before we arrived at the venue, and Rahn and I were waiting for the five-minute cue from the production team for Barbara to go backstage for a last-minute touch-up. I was standing alone—Rahn had stepped away—when Larry Gatlin, of the Gatlin Brothers Band, came over to say hello. I think he had a bit of a crush on me. He shook my hand, placing something in it! "See you later!" he said and left me standing there. I wasn't sure what was in my hand—I didn't dare look—and when Rahn came back, I told him about the exchange. Then I shook his hand and passed "it" on, like a hot potato. He took one quick look at the "gift" and said, "Oh shit!" It was a bag of cocaine, and there were Secret Service men everywhere. So what was a guy to do? "I'll be right back," he said, and he tracked down the original gifter, shook his hand, and gave it back! Thank God!

I had barely recovered my composure when a production assistant came up to give us the five-minute warning. I needed to let Barbara know. She was right behind me, so I turned quickly and said, "Barb!" at which point Mrs. Bush turned to me and replied, "Yes?"

Again, I was completely flustered. "I'm so sorry, Mrs. Bush; I was trying to get Barbara Mandrell's attention."

I must have blushed fifteen different shades of red, but Mrs. Bush could not have been lovelier and immediately put me at my ease. "Not a problem," she laughed.

So much for my singular moment with "Barb," the First Lady of the United States!

•   •   •

All during the late 1970s and early 1980s, when we were on the road, the tour bus was our dressing room. It was a beautiful vehicle, kind of rose color and gray, very modern, with a nice kitchen and bathroom and sleeping bunks for the people who would travel with Barbara. Sometimes it was the kids with the nanny if it was summertime or her road manager or someone from her management company. Then there was a second band bus that carried all the musicians and their instruments.

The main bus was also a traveling dressing room. When Barbara played in some of the smaller venues around the country, I would meet the bus when it arrived, and we would do her makeup and hair on the bus. Of course, when we were in Nashville at the Opry or the Country Music Awards, they had sizeable dressing rooms. Because I was around the country scene so much with Barbara, I was recognized, and soon I was being greeted like an old friend. The people were always warm and friendly and made me feel right at home. To be honest, I was having the time of my life!

When we went to Nashville for Fan Fair, I realized just how big a star Barbara was. Fan Fair is where all the celebrities come out and meet their fans and maybe sing a song or two. It's an annual event, and it's a big thing with the fan clubs. Being in the midst of that kind of fan worship was really crazy. One time I had to go to the bathroom, and some of the fans followed me there. While I was in the stall, they were asking, "Can I have one of her powder puffs?" I was like, really? But that was the kind of stuff they would do, because this was their life. These are die-hard fans of people in show business. It's not very different from the avid basketball or football fans who paint their faces or dye their hair the team colors. These fans will do anything for the stars they worship. They write letters, and they draw pictures and send photos. You have no idea the stuff that Barbara would get as gifts from the fans, and when she was in Nashville the adoration was so intense that it was slightly insane. Over the years Barbara collected so much memorabilia from her fans and from her work that for quite a while there was a Barbara Mandrell Museum in Nashville to house all her memorabilia, costumes, and fan paraphernalia.

In 1983 after two grueling years on the *Barbara Mandrell and the Mandrell Sisters* TV show, Barbara took another big step and premiered a Las Vegas stage show, *The Lady Is a Champ*. She was now truly a major star—headlining on the Vegas Strip with her own band in an act that included a group of gospel singers and a troupe of dancers. Once again, her trusty dance partner was Vince Paterson.

Life with Barbara was exciting, and I enjoyed the time we had together in Vegas. I would go there and stay with her for two weeks at a time. It was such a different life, staying up late and sleeping into part of the day. I had no idea I could do that. It wasn't in my wheelhouse. I felt like a completely different person. Mitch would come up with the kids, and sometimes my mom came as well. We tried to hold onto some semblance of normalcy, and on Thanksgiving we all shared a wonderful dinner with Barbara and her family, but living in Las Vegas was truly other-worldly.

In 1983, when Barbara and her sisters were taping in Los Angeles, I decided to throw a Halloween party for my husband, Mitch, in honor of his fortieth birthday. The guests were asked to come in spectacular costumes. Barbara and her dance partner, Vince Paterson, came as Little Red Riding Hood and the Big Bad Wolf. Patty Duke came as a puppy. Mitch was Captain Hook, and I was Elvira. One couple came as Rubik's cubes. Another couple came as the Coneheads. My friend Patti did a good job as Elizabeth Taylor, and Randy Fuhrman, who catered this and many other parties for us, was a spectacular Carmen Miranda. We had Mickey and Minnie, the Devil and his Angels, but the two most creative were "Shit Faced with a Buzz On," she in a bee costume with simulated poo on her face and he in a "flasher" overcoat with a dildo coming out of his shorts—it actually moved about in circles, and the crowd went wild over it! My mother had the time of her life; she laughed louder and longer than anyone! All the guests were wonderfully creative, and I remember this as one of my most successful parties ever.

As the Mandrell show climbed in the ratings, Barbara and her husband, Ken Dudney, built a mansion outside Nashville, in a very beautiful wooded area. They almost had their own forest! At that time, it was the largest log home ever built, and, yep, it included a helicopter pad. Ken had been a navy carrier pilot and had flown for four governors of Tennessee. Whenever I flew to Nashville, Ken would be at the airport with the helicopter to fly me to their home. I would white-knuckle it each and every time. Looking back, I can appreciate what a skilled pilot Ken was and what a great way it was to get where I was going.

Then in 1984, at the peak of Barbara Mandell's popularity, every-thing came to a halt when she was hit by a wrong-way driver in a head-on car crash that almost ended her career. Her two children were in the car with her. Fortunately, they all survived, but the injuries they sustained would take many months of recovery. The driver of the other car was not so lucky; he was killed in the crash.

Barbara had a brain injury, among other things, and this brain injury impacted her in a lot of ways. Recovery was a slow process, and for a long time she couldn't even see herself as Barbara Mandrell. Barbara Walters interviewed her in Nashville sometime after the accident. The day before the interview, I was in Barbara's bedroom, sitting at the side of her bed, when she said, "I don't want to be her."

I said, "You don't want to be who?"

"I don't want to be Barbara Mandrell."

"Who do you want to be?"

"I want to be Barbara Dudney."

She had been married to her husband, Ken, since she was a young girl, and their solid marriage was the foundation of her life. Now there were so many things wrong with her from the accident that all she wanted to do was be a wife and mother. I realized that fear, depression, and trauma had deeply affected her normally determined spirit and that it would take time for her to regain what she had so brutally lost.

"That's going to change," I said. "You'll see. It's going to take awhile. You're hurting now, but that's going to change."

And, slowly, it did. I think the television interview with Barbara Walters was incredibly hard for her, and I was glad to be there to support her. That healing process and all that we shared during that time brought us closer together. The one bright spot during her recovery was that she became pregnant with her third child, Nathan, who added so much joy to her life.

It took a year and a half for her to recover, and once she did, her desire to perform returned, and she came back as strong as ever. She did a lot of guest-star performances on television, some of which I worked on and some of which I didn't, because of my union situation. In 1990 she wrote her autobiography, *Get to the Heart: My Story*. We went all over the country on a promotional tour for the book. I did her makeup for all the interviews with Oprah, Sally Jessy Raphael, the *Tonight Show*, and the other big talk shows.

Once again Barbara was topping the record charts and touring and performing with the same intensity as she had done in previous years.

In 1997 Hallmark and Mandalay Television produced the TV movie *Get to The Heart: The Barbara Mandrell Story*, in which my daughter, Portia, played her sister Louise and Jaime Dudney, Barbara's real-life daughter, portrayed her other sister, Irlene.

The making of that film seemed to bring Barbara full circle. That year she officially retired. My guess is she quit, or retired, because she'd had enough of the grind of having to put herself out there every day, of having to be "on." I think now she was truly ready to just be Barbara Dudney. I don't think a day goes by she isn't happy that she made that decision.

* * *

From what I've observed, working with so many female stars, I don't think a lot of pretty women are very excited about getting older in front of the public. It's not the way they want to be remembered, and they don't want people to think, "Wow, what happened to her?" (unless, of course, you are an actress like Meryl Streep, where you play to that). I think that wanting to have a home life was something Barbara had been craving for a long time, and the first several years of her retirement have been incredibly creative and artistic. She made a garden like you've never seen. And then she started making pottery with beautiful designs that went into the garden. Her artistry is amazing. She's a super talented human being, and that hasn't changed.

15

STAR LIGHT,
STAR BRIGHT

*If you concentrate on finding whatever
is good in every situation, you will discover
that your life will suddenly be filled with
gratitude—a feeling that nurtures the soul.*

—RABBI HAROLD KUSHNER

Although I worked with a lot of country music artists, I also
worked with celebrities in many other diverse fields. Mohammed
Ali was one of my favorites. We were working on an automobile
commercial that was set somewhere in the Middle East, but the
actual shoot took place at a remote location way northeast of Los
Angeles on one of the dry lakes in the Mojave Desert. In other words,
nowheresville. Ali had arrived in a helicopter, and because I drove
the nicest car in the group, I was sent to pick him up. He was warm
and friendly. This was before there were any signs of his oncoming
struggle with Parkinson's disease and dementia. He had a very playful
personality, and everyone on the set was incredibly excited to be in
his presence. As the day progressed, children seemed to appear out of
nowhere. He became the Pied Piper of all the local kids, hugging them

and playing at fighting with them. I'll never forget him: a-larger-than-life personality with the gentleness of a lamb.

Working with photographer Dick Zimmerman gave me the opportunity to meet a lot of famous and fabulous people. Dick photographed Mel Brooks for the cover of *Los Angeles Magazine* to promote the movie *High Anxiety*. Patti Altbaum was the stylist and had to tie Mel into a straight-jacket. We all howled with laughter as Mel did all kinds of shtick while he was being strapped into it. Many years later Mitch and I went to the Annenberg Center for the Performing Arts to see Mel give a talk, and we were fortunate enough to go backstage after the performance. When I mentioned to him that I'd done his makeup those many years ago, he was gracious enough to take a picture of us together.

I also worked on a promotion for the phenomenally successful television show *Mork and Mindy*. Working with Robin Williams was a true privilege. I expected him to be hilariously funny, as he was in the show, or at least very animated, as he was in interviews, but he turned out to be quiet and refined. I spent a whole day with him, and it is indelibly etched in my memory.

Tom Jones was hot as a pistol at that time, with many hit records to his name. He was definitely cute and sexy, and if the bulge in his pants wasn't a sock, it was definitely something oversized! Difficult to concentrate on the makeup!

I did makeup for many men, including Eddie Arnold, John Davidson, and Richard Crenna, all big television stars at the time. However, the one genuine movie star who stood out head and shoulders above them all, and who made me most nervous, was Paul Newman, another one who definitely falls into the hot category!

He was gorgeous—relaxed and down-to-earth, casually sipping on a beer, probably laughing inside as he watched this very nervous makeup artist try to act cool while freaking out inside. He was very kind and tried to put me at ease, even though I was dying of fear.

Needless to say, working on men is quite different from working on women. Usually, I just had to even out their complexion, cover up blemishes and dark circles under their eyes, give them a bit of color, and groom their brows. Every now and then I would work on someone who was very light-complexioned and needed a bit of eyeliner and a dab of mascara just to make their eyes show up in the photograph.

I worked on a couple of album covers for the Village People, who were enjoying a series of hits and were immensely popular. We always had a good time together. All the band members were Americans, but the group had been formed to target disco's gay audience by French producers Jacques Morali and Henri Belolo. They were best known for their on-stage costumes, catchy tunes, and suggestive lyrics. They were really nice guys. One day I mentioned that my son played Little League baseball and asked whether they would like to do something for the team. They ended up sponsoring the team and even came to one of the games. That was a pretty fabulous gesture, and one I'll always be grateful for.

Of course, I worked mostly with women, such as Priscilla Presley, she of the luminous skin and beautiful eyes. We worked together a couple of times, and many years later I ran into her at a brunch in the Malibu home of Fred Hayman, who started Georgio's Boutique on Rodeo Drive in Beverly Hills. It was there that celebrities and movie folk came in droves to peruse the latest fashions hot off the runway. There was a bar and pool table in the boutique to entertain the husbands and boyfriends while their women shopped for beautiful clothes. It was a favorite place for actors and actresses to dress in one-of-a-kind designs, created by Fred and his minions, for their red-carpet appearances at the Oscars and Emmys. Fred is the true godfather of the Rodeo Drive phenomenon, heading the Rodeo Drive Committee, which brought in high-end European labels to Beverly Hills. The Rodeo Drive we know today, which attracts tourists from all over the world, owes its beginnings to this great innovator, who truly loved the city of Beverly Hills and was beloved by all. Once I'd reminded Priscilla that I'd done her makeup, we spent most of the afternoon just chatting away. She was very forthcoming and down to earth.

I was getting my nails done one day when I looked up and saw a woman staring at me. It took me a moment to realize it was Paula Abdul. Interestingly enough, people have often remarked that she and I look very much alike. She must have thought the same thing, and we exchanged a look that said, "I know. People think we look alike!" We then engaged in a conversation that lasted the duration of our manicures, and by the time we'd finished, we had become fast friends. We exchanged phone numbers, and soon after, she called to make an appointment for a makeup lesson. She wanted to try some new colors. Just before the appointment, she called crying that she couldn't make it because her best friend was in the hospital. "No problem. We can do it another time," I said. It took two other scheduled and canceled appointments for her to show up. Finally, I gave her a makeup lesson, and she bought a lot of product, but that was the last I heard of my new best friend Paula.

One of my favorite celebrity stories happened when my hair-dresser friend Rahn McDow and I flew out of town to work on Barbara Mandrell for a television special in which she was to guest-star with international singing sensation Julio Iglesias. A van picked us up at the airport, together with others who were working on the show, and it turned out that one of the passengers was one of Julio's people. He was a particularly charming Italian guy with lots of personality. We arrived on the set just as Julio was stepping out of the elevator, and Mr. Charm kindly introduced us. We arrived back at the airport the following day, having done the show, to find Julio and Mr. Charm also getting their belongings out of their car. Suddenly, Julio ran right up to me, kissed me smack-dab on the mouth, and said, "Nice meeting you." Then he ran back to his friend, who was laughing his head off. I'm sure he put Julio up to it. I didn't know what hit me! I know that nowadays that might be considered crossing a line, but Julio was so hot and incredibly sexy all I could do was smile at my good fortune.

* * *

When I was dating Mitch, he would tell me about some of his clients—among them, Patty Duke and John Astin. In those days everyone knew who Patty Duke was, though she preferred to be called by her birth name, Anna. She had received an Academy Award for her portrayal of Helen Keller in *The Miracle Worker* (the youngest actress at the time to win an Oscar); she was the star of her own show, *The Patty Duke Show*, in which she played rival cousins; and she was one of the stars of the hugely successful film *The Valley of the Dolls*. Her husband, John Astin, was best known for his portrayal of Gomez Addams in the television show *The Addams Family*.

Mitch knew we would all get along—our kids were close to the same age—and he arranged for us all to meet, starting a friendship that was to last for many years. Mitch and I did notice there were some issues between Patty and John, but, then, almost every couple has issues, and we never commented or interfered. We enjoyed many Christmas holidays together with our families at their house.

Before long Anna asked if I would make her up for her new television series, *It Takes Two*. The stars, along with Patty Duke, were Richard Crenna, Billie Bird, Helen Hunt, and Anthony Edwards. The latter two played Patty and Dick's children. Hard to believe they ever were so young!

The producers offered me the position of head makeup artist on the show, but, again, because I wasn't in the union, they had to hire a union makeup artist as a standby. I had never done makeup on a television sitcom, and this turned out to be another example of jumping into something I really wasn't qualified for. Fortunately, one of the union makeup artists was so incredibly generous in helping me understand what my job was that I ended up doing the makeup for Anna, Billy Bird, and Helen Hunt every week. The actors also had to do a lot of PR for the show, and I did all their makeup for these sessions. Anna usually liked very simple, natural makeup, but for this show she allowed me to make her look as glamorous as possible. It wasn't very difficult!

When *It Takes Two* went off the air, Anna was cast in another sitcom, *Hail to the Chief,* in which she played the president of the United States and Ted Bessell played her husband. I worked on this sitcom as well. The series was lots of fun but lasted only one season.

It is now well known that Patty suffered a horrendous childhood. Her alcoholic father and her clinically depressed mother turned her life over to her then-agents, John and Ethel Ross, when she was eight years old. The Ross's recognized her talent and looked upon her as a potential cash cow. They billed her as two years younger than she actually was and plied her with alcohol and prescription drugs. They took more than their legal share of commissions, and, to cap it all off, they made sexual advances on her. Her life became chaotic: numerous affairs with inappropriate men and, eventually, four marriages. She had been having a high-profile relationship with Desi Arnaz Jr. when in 1970 she became pregnant—not by Desi but by a man by the name of Michael Tell, whom she immediately married, though the marriage did not last a year. Eventually, she married John Astin, with whom she had another child. It was a good marriage—while it lasted.

Anna and I became very close while we were working together. She confided in me that she was seeing a psychiatrist and that during the taping of *It Takes Two* she was diagnosed with manic depression, which is now referred to as bipolar disorder. She was treated for this challenging condition, and thereafter, she devoted much of her time to advocating for and educating the public on mental health issues. She needed to effect change, to put a face on the disease and bring it out of the closet. Shortly after Anna's diagnosis, she and John split up, a sad day for all who knew and loved them.

Eventually, Anna met Michael Pearce, a drill sergeant who was consulting on a movie she was shooting. They moved to Idaho, where Pearce worked as a firefighter. In my mind, this was the first and only time she could live a normal life as Anna Marie Pearce, a regular, happily married woman. They asked Mitch to help them adopt a child, Kevin, to complete their family. She abandoned a lot of her Hollywood relationships when she moved to Idaho, but I don't think she regretted it for a moment. Anna was a good person who raised beautiful and talented children. She and her family have a special place in my heart, forever.

. . .

With most of these stars, it was just a matter of making them look good on camera. They had already established their own looks, so it was different from the way I worked with the country music artists, where I had more latitude. For example, a record company would say, "We want you to do a makeover on her. We want her to look "different," and that's what you see in the before and after pictures of Barbara Mandrell and Tammy Wynette: no longer country in the least bit, but hip and modern. That was the most fun for me. And the best thing was how excited and thrilled the country artists were. Both Barbara and Tammy went out and bought fabulous clothes and changed their whole look; they became obsessed with fashion. I didn't do that for Dolly Parton because she had her own style. We just improved upon it. Barbara and Tammy were country when country wasn't cool. Then they became country cool.

I generally didn't like putting a lot of makeup on people. With most celebrities I preferred a more natural look. They'd tell me what they wanted, and I'd say, "OK, that's fine, but let's do it in a way that you stand out and don't fade into the picture." And then when I was done, I'd take a Polaroid and let them see it. Every once in a while, someone would panic and say "Oh, my God, it's too much." That's when the photographer would get involved. He'd say, "It's not too much, because when I put the lighting and filter on you . . ." That was how we made it work, as a team effort, which is something most people don't understand about Hollywood. They think it's all about the stars. Of course, the stars are important, but what makes Hollywood truly great is that it's a collaboration of some of the most talented artists on earth, working together in every aspect of the filmmaking process to create the magic that we see on the screen. Even with all the pressure to be a perfectionist, the tough schedules (often fifteen- to seventeen-hour days), and the demanding people and personalities, it's still a privilege to work in that heady atmosphere and a pleasure to get to do that for a living! At least it was, until it wasn't

Jane Seymour promo picture for Somewhere in Time, 1980 (courtesy of Dick Zimmerman Photography)

Priscilla Presley (courtesy of Dick Zimmerman Photography)

Stockard Channing (courtesy of Dick Zimmerman Photography)

One of Shari Belafonte's favorite photographic portraits (courtesy of Dick Broun Photography)

131

*Robin Williams during his Mork and Mindy days
(courtesy of Dick Zimmerman Photography)*

*Tom Jones in an iconic pose (courtesy
of Dick Zimmerman Photography)*

Album cover for the Village People, 1980

Nicolette Sheridan (courtesy of Dick Zimmerman Photography)

133

Barbara Sinatra standing in front of many of Frank Sinatra's awards. She was chairman of her own golf tournament to benefit children in Palm Springs. (courtesy of Matthew Rolston)

US Synchronized Swimming team at the 1992 Olympics in Barcelona, Spain. They brought home the gold!

16

ONE DOOR CLOSES

*Beauty begins the moment you
decide to be yourself.*

—COCO CHANEL

In the 1990s I realized my career had become much greater than I ever thought possible. Not only was I working with some of the best photographers but also I was actually creating looks for some of the most famous faces in Hollywood. I was also on and off airplanes, dragging my bags everywhere and constantly staying at different hotels, plus I was dealing with producers who weren't happy with having to pay me more than the union artists. It was exhausting and stressful, but I understood that eventually my life as a freelance artist would come to an end. I later realized that I could use all that makeup experience to design a second line of cosmetics that would carry me for the next twenty years. But, for now, I was still on a roll.

In 1991 I was flown to New York City for a photo shoot with Dolly, and I stayed at the Pierre hotel, very close to her apartment, which she shared at the time with her manager, Sandy Gallin. He occupied one wing of the apartment, and Dolly occupied the other, sharing the central living quarters. It was a spectacular apartment across from Central Park and was beautifully designed and decorated. In fact, I took notes on the decor and used that apartment as an inspiration to decorate my own home.

I was in the living room, waiting for Dolly to call me in, when Sandy Gallin walked out of his bedroom in his underwear, looking around to see what was going on. I'd met him many times before, but I'm not sure he knew who I was in these surroundings. He didn't seem at all put out that I was sitting there watching him walk about in his tighty-whities! I just pretended this was the most normal thing in the world, smiled, and nodded hello.

Dolly and I went off to the photo shoot, where we learned that Julia Roberts was working in the next studio. Julia and Dolly had worked together on the movie *Steel Magnolias* back in the 1980s, so Julia came in to say hi. She warned us to be very watchful as we left the studio because the street was filled with paparazzi. When we were ready to leave, we had the limo pull as far into the building as possible so we wouldn't be seen. The limo had tinted windows, and the paparazzi swarmed around. Dolly said they probably thought it was Julia Roberts's limo, and they followed us uptown all the way to Dolly's apartment. We drove down into the parking garage, where the paparazzi were not allowed, but they followed us anyway. We parked, and Dolly told us, "You guys wait here. I'll get out first." The paparazzi immediately surrounded the car, cameras at the ready, surprised to see Dolly emerge and race toward the elevator singing, "I'm not Julia. My name is Dolly!" It's not often you see a shocked expression on the faces of the paparazzi!

All through the 1980s and early 1990s, Bob Hope was the king of television specials, and Barbara Mandrell performed in more than a few of his shows. One special birthday show, it might have been his eightieth, took place on an aircraft carrier in St. Petersburg, Florida. It was a star-studded show: Elizabeth Taylor, Sammy Davis Jr., and, of course, Barbara Mandrell. I was out on the deck, watching rehearsals. I looked to my left and saw Sammy Davis Jr. sitting alone. Hoping he might remember my dad, I thought it would be nice to tell him my dad had always spoken so highly of him. I introduced myself and told him my dad had worked with him many times. When I told him my dad's name, he immediately exclaimed, "Label?" My dad's name was Lou—Label in Yiddish. Only people who knew my dad well called him Label. We had an immediate rapport, and Sammy couldn't have been nicer.

Everyone working on the show on the aircraft carrier had to pass through the hair, makeup, and wardrobe room in order to get to the outside deck. At one point, we were all—including Barbara—told that we would have to leave the room when Elizabeth Taylor walked through. I'd never been in the company of a star who required all the underlings to be removed from their sight! That was a first!

All in all, having a front-row seat for some of the most renowned entertainers in the world, on an aircraft carrier to boot, was something I'll always remember. As it turned out, after the taping Barbara; her husband, Ken; Sammy Davis; and I wound up waiting at the airport together. Being in close proximity to so much incredible talent and passing the time together like friends . . . well, what can I say? It was one of my favorite days.

I don't know whether it was coincidence or my meeting with Sammy Davis Jr., but shortly after, I received a call from a friend who was working for Barbara Sinatra. She wanted to know whether I was available to do Barbara's makeup for a big event. Frank Sinatra was very ill at that time. I went to their home but never did lay eyes on him. Sadly, he died only a week or so later. I began to work with Barbara at her homes in Beverly Hills and Malibu. She was a lovely woman, very professional, with the most exquisite jewelry. She would show me her outfit for a specific event, and I always asked what jewels she was planning to wear so I could enhance her green eyes. Her emeralds were beyond fabulous!

Barbara hosted a charity golf tournament every year in Palm Springs, and I did her makeup for all the promotional material. One year I was thrilled to hear that Kirk Douglas was the honoree, and Barbara asked me to help him with his makeup. Not gonna lie—I was thrilled! He was, after all, an icon. He was charming and put me at ease right away.

Barbara also recommended me to Jeanne Martin, Dean Martin's former wife and mother of three of his children. Interestingly, there were numerous photographs of the very handsome Dean all over the house. It was obvious she never stopped loving him.

So: Sammy Davis Jr., Barbara Sinatra, and the former Mrs. Dean Martin. I couldn't help feeling that my dad orchestrated this as a remembrance of all the recordings he did with Sinatra, Davis, and Martin, some of the greatest superstars of the music world.

One of the sidebars of working with these wonderful people is they attract some of the best people in the world to work with them, and then you get to work with the best people. Of course, that means that you always have to be careful not to overstep your bounds, because creative people are very sensitive about their work and their careers and you have to be very respectful in how you communicate with them. It's an important part of navigating the unspoken but very real caste system in show business.

I was really good friends with Bill Hargate, the multi-Emmy Award-winning designer who did the wardrobe on Barbara Mandrell's show. We would talk about the colors and the look. He was amazing, always open to discussing details, and never made me feel that I stepped on his toes in any way. Rahn McDow, who was the hairdresser for Barbara and her sisters, was also a friend, so Bill Hargate, Rahn, and I would discuss the look we were going for. I always believed that my job was to make Barbara look good, and I was very honest with her and told her from the beginning, "If you want me to tell you the truth, I'm going to." I had no qualms about saying, "That's ugly; take it off" or "I don't like your hair like that; tell him to pull it down over here." I was always looking in the camera, and I'd see something and say, "Here, you need these earrings." I'd take them off myself and put them on her. I did a lot of that with Barbara, Tammy Wynette, and others. But I always did it as a friend; it was what you would do if you were a friend to somebody. Sometimes in a professional situation people are hesitant to say anything to celebrities because they are intimidated. It was professional, but I also felt, why should I allow them to not look good? If there's nobody else around that's going to tell them the truth, I'm going to—and they appreciated it.

Dolly Parton was a different story. I never had to tell her anything. She had her own style and knew exactly what she wanted. And she's great, a fabulous woman. She's well traveled, knows everybody, knows how to comport herself in different situations. She's clever and funny. She has it all going for her, and she's always herself. I mean, she has the smarts to know what to say and how to say it, and she's pretty much who she is. I never found her affected in the least. No pretentiousness at all—none. I've been all over with her, in a lot of situations—Vegas, New York, Nashville. "Hi, y'all" is who she is, even with her fans.

Both Dolly and Barbara Mandrell were really warm and friendly with their fans. They're truly sweet when they're out there, but when they're done, they're done, and they need to leave. But they never want to leave a bad taste in a fan's mouth. They're likeable women and they do what they need to do for people to keep liking them. Sometimes I would be the heavy—not so much for Dolly but for Barbara. I knew both of them so well that I knew when they'd had enough. Even though I was a makeup artist, I knew when I needed to jump in and move things along. It's another one of those skills you learn on the job that has nothing to do with being a good makeup artist and everything to do with being a valuable part of the team.

In 1998 I did the job with Dolly that I am most proud of: a Christmas television movie, *Unlikely Angel*. It was a film that would hold up over the years and continues to be played during the holiday season. When I took the assignment, I had no idea that it would mark an important turning point in my life.

In the movie Dolly portrayed a country music performer who meets an untimely demise but cannot enter heaven until she performs a good deed back on earth: to get a workaholic widower and his children back together again for Christmas. The fun for me was that I got to make her up as both Angel Dolly and Dolly Dolly. Angel Dolly was soft and pretty and ethereal looking, which was a wonderful way for me to express how I often saw her. Most of the film was shot on location, some of it way out in the boonies. We shot the interiors in an old bar, and after dinner we would shoot the exteriors in the freezing, freezing cold.

Dolly, trooper that she is, never complained once. But even with layers and layers of clothing, nothing could keep me warm. We wrapped at 5:00 a.m. I was scared to death driving home on the dark and unfamiliar icy roads. We had no cell phones then, no MapQuest or Waze. I was out there completely on my own with no idea what I would do if I slid off the road or had an accident. I didn't enjoy the feeling of being so vulnerable and afraid. Finally, the last night on the way home, I began to cry. I just didn't want to do this anymore.

I was done working on these crazy locations all over the country, at all hours of the day and night, and in all kinds of inclement weather. This would be my last movie shoot. Upon returning home I told Mitch I was done. I was going to quit.

It all made sense at the time. I was fifty-four years old, my kids were grown and gone. Barbara Mandrell was going to retire to become what she had always wanted to be, a wife and mother. My other freelance photography work was slowing down, and after the Dolly movie it seemed like the right time to say, "I'm done."

∙ ∙ ∙

Fortunately, my husband, Mitch, supported me in whatever decision I came to, and at first, my retirement seemed like a welcome change. I was involved in the requisite activities retired people do: shopping, having lunch with friends, enjoying a full social life, and spending more time with my family. Unfortunately, the downside of it was I was bored. After a few months of enjoying my newfound freedom, my creative side started nudging me: "You can't just sit around like this, doing nothing!" I needed something new and exciting to fill my days. But what did I want to do? I was struggling to figure that out.

At one point my girlfriend Gayle and I decided we were going to become diet counselors. That didn't last very long. Cheerleading women who were struggling to lose one pound in two months didn't quite have the same joy that came from making women look beautiful in a forty-five-minute makeup session. I had to admit that makeup was what I knew and what I loved.

I talked it over with Mitch and told him I wanted to take the skills I already had and open myself up to doing something more unique with them. I wasn't sure what that was exactly, but I decided to go to a couple of cosmetic shows and see what was going on in the makeup world.

That's what I did, and what I saw there was exciting. People were coming up with new ways of mixing ingredients and creating new looks. I came back with all that artistic inspiration saying, "I can create something even cooler than I did last time," and that's when I got the idea to open my own makeup store in Beverly Hills.

I started by talking about it to anyone who would listen. Some of my friends thought I was crazy. Why would I want to open a retail business at my age? Several people said I wouldn't last. Many thought it would be too expensive. One day I mentioned the idea to my neighbor. He was a bit skeptical and asked, "Why do you want to do such a risky thing?"

"I just feel like I should do it," I replied.

His wife, who was a super shopper, suggested, "Maybe you should think about doing it on South Beverly Drive, because they don't have much there." She was the kind of woman who wouldn't buy anything that didn't have a designer label on it, but I thought that she was on to something.

South Beverly Drive was more of a neighborhood kind of place where people who lived south of Wilshire Boulevard shopped. You had the cleaners, the drug store, and the children's store—which you also had north of Wilshire, but here a cup of coffee didn't cost five dollars. This was the more affordable side of Beverly Hills. There were a lot of food places where you could go and grab a sandwich, whereas north of Wilshire Boulevard you had to "dine" rather than "grab and go."

The very next day I went looking on South Beverly Drive and found a perfect spot on the east side of the street, dead center of the block at a crosswalk—which was fabulous because wherever people wanted to go, they had to cross in front of that store.

I talked to Mitch about it and said, "I really think I can do this." Without missing a beat, he said, "OK. Go for it!" And just like that, I began a whole new creative phase of my life, the Bobbe Joy Makeup Studio.

17

THE BOBBE JOY
MAKEUP STUDIO

*The best color in the world is the
one that looks best on you.*

—COCO CHANEL

"Necessity is the mother of invention." I never really knew the full meaning of that saying until I was in the middle of a photo shoot or television show and suddenly realized I didn't have certain colors I needed. I always enjoyed the challenge of coming up with quick, creative solutions. I would dive into my makeup kit and start mixing different products to arrive at a color or a texture I needed. Before long I became very adept at this kind of makeup wizardry. So the idea of creating a makeup line was not foreign to me. But I wanted more; I wanted to bring something new and innovative to the marketplace.

In 1998 the Bobbe Joy Makeup Studio opened on South Beverly Drive in Beverly Hills. It was a great location, and I was very particular about how I wanted the store to look. I designed it in a way that was really pretty and had a nice flow. The floors were done in big slate tiles that were multicolored, so that if any makeup fell on them, you wouldn't see it. In the front was a comfortable sofa and a desk, and everything was curved. All the wood was a warm cherry tone, and the walls were painted a soft peach (the most flattering color for skin tones). But it was also a very functional space. I had curved shelves installed along the back wall with gift items and a back room where we could do waxing, and another back area I used for storage. In the main area there were three really pretty curved makeup stations, and on the other side was a wall with glass display shelves entirely filled with makeup and a glass display case that held every makeup sample available: bottles, jars, testers of everything. People could come in and try whatever they wanted with help from the staff.

The makeup line I was creating was very contemporary and true to fashion but also could be utilized by any age or any style, hip or conservative. I didn't want to just have the coolest, youngest thing; I had to have something for everyone. We were customizing our foundations for different skin types, tones, and textures. A client would come in, and I would look at her and say her skin was dry, or oily, or whatever, and I would mix a special foundation, either oil free or with oil, just for her. Depending on her age I might put some pearl essence in it, because it would give her more of a glow, which we lack as we get older. Custom blending became a huge attraction of the store.

Even though there are hundreds of makeup bases for people to choose from, my foundations were made for women who had difficulty finding the right makeup for their skin. I sourced a company that manufactured pigments, frosts, bases, and additives to create lipsticks and lip glosses from scratch. Many cosmetic companies discontinued favorite lip colors in order to motivate the customer to buy a new lipstick color line, and I realized I could make my own recipes to re-create the discontinued colors. I also made a rainbow of lipsticks and glosses that were unique to my own label. The ingredients were of the highest quality, and the colors would never be discontinued, even if we removed them from the line: the recipes would always be there to revive. The only negative was that this work was very intensive. Only four lipsticks could be poured at one time, and for lip glosses we were lucky if we got two out of one batch. I purchased the colors and did the mixing in the shop right in front of the client. Customers could also play with all the testers on their own, like in a department store, or the women who worked for me would help them make the right choices. They'd say, "Sit down here. I'll show you how to do this" or "Come here and I'll put this color on you."

My theory was, "People will buy if you help them," not "People will buy if you try to jam it down their throat." I just could never do that. Someone once said to me, "You're a *negative* salesperson, because you tell people they don't need *that*, but they *should* get this." She was right. That is what I would say. I had discovered from all the years of working in the celebrity makeup business that people generally appreciate honesty if it's going to make them look more beautiful or more handsome. And it's all in the way you say it. I learned how to be diplomatic while being honest at the same time.

I know that I owe a great deal of my success to the fact that I am naturally a people person. I enjoyed hearing what other people had to say and always felt comfortable giving my honest opinion. That helped establish long-term relationships of trust and confidence, which had a positive effect on my business. Often, I had clients who would tell me what they wanted, and I would give them advice on why that would or wouldn't work.

I had clients who insisted they had to have red lipstick. We'd have a discussion. Number one, we had to get the right red lipstick. Number two, you can't have as bold an eye if you're going to wear red lipstick. You're going to look like your lips and eyes are coming in the door before you do. You don't want to look painted. You want to see all of you coming in the door at the same time. You want people to look at you and say, "Wow, look what an attractive woman she is." Not, "Oh my God, look at all that makeup." If you're wearing a red lip, that's fine, but you've got to be careful what you do with the rest of your face. You have to know how to balance your face correctly, the same way you balance your body by choosing your wardrobe correctly—what to emphasize and what to play down.

I was always telling my clients, "Don't buy that. You already have twenty-seven of those" or "Why are you buying that color? It's totally wrong for you." My clients definitely appreciated my candor. I wanted the Bobbe Joy Makeup Studio to be a place without pretense, a place that people would enjoy coming to—and they did.

When I opened the store, I had two people working for me, and that was it: a young woman who had worked for Senna Cosmetics and my daughter, Portia. Then slowly I hired a third makeup artist, and then I hired a PR firm, Harris Shepherd Public Relations, and that's when things really got going. I appeared on QVC with a line of eyebrow products and appeared in lots of segments on the morning and afternoon talk shows.

It was great having my daughter, Portia, work for me. At that time she was establishing a solid career as an actress in television and films. But as with all actors, there are slow times. This job gave her another creative outlet, and was she ever creative! Her lipstick making and talent for eye-catching displays were definitely an asset to the business.

With my background at Jon Peters and all the work I had done with major stars and top-name photographers, I had enough interesting stories to give the publicists a lot to work with— plus in me they had a client with a big mouth who loved to talk about her store. I got into all the fashion and beauty magazines. As a result, I started getting more and more business and had to hire more and more makeup artists.

At certain times we were all very busy with clients, but when we weren't, I had the other women making customized lipsticks or lip glosses, and they would make them right there where people could sit and watch. We made them from scratch, so if people liked a certain lip color and they couldn't find it anywhere, they would bring their old one in and I could match it perfectly. Word of our very specialized services began to spread, and our reputation as a unique makeup studio grew steadily. We were named Best Brows in Los Angeles by *Los Angeles* magazine and *Allure* magazine, Best Makeup lesson in L.A. by *Shape* magazine, and the renowned *GAYOT Guide to the Best in L.A. and Southern California* wrote, "Bobbe Joy brings makeup to a high art form." I couldn't have imagined a higher compliment.

I hadn't done makeup on anyone but models and celebrities for the past twenty years, yet when I opened the Bobbe Joy Makeup Studio, my favorite clients were always those who had nothing to do with celebrity. They were just interesting men (yes, men!) and women of all ages and ethnicities whose anecdotes and words of wisdom filled my days with unexpected joy. Most of all, I loved my therapist clients because I could either pick their brain or become their therapist while they sat in my chair. I'm sure I used my fifty-plus years of talking to women to give them some good advice while also receiving pearls of wisdom from them.

Many of my longtime celebrity clients did become regular customers, but the one who always sent shock waves through the Bobbe Joy Makeup Studio was Dolly Parton. She would come into the shop unexpectedly and announce: "Hi, Bobbe, I want some makeup!"

The other makeup artists and their clients would practically have heart attacks! Sometimes Jason Pirro, Dolly's longtime assistant and driver, would call in advance and say, "Dolly's coming in. Is there a place to park in the back?" I would have one of the girls move my car so they could pull in. Dolly would come in the back way and hang out and get whatever makeup she needed. It was always fun when she stopped by.

Many of my other celebrity clients came by on a regular basis to buy products or to get their brows or makeup done. Mila Kunis was a regular eyebrow client. Sometimes she came in with her then-boy-friend, Macaulay Culkin, who loved hanging out with us. Another eyebrow client was Lily Collins. Her mom, Jill, and I were on the Greystone Foundation board together. I mentioned to Jill that Lily had the most spectacular eyebrows—she was about thirteen at the time. I begged Jill to let me shape them when Lily was ready, because I was afraid others might make them too thin. I started shaping Lily's brows when she was about fifteen and even used her as a model for a pre-Oscar television show on the subject of eyebrows.

Some of the celebrities who came to the studio were particularly memorable. Cheryl Howard, Ron Howard's wife, came in a few times to get her makeup done for some special events and award shows. Ron would sit patiently, reading scripts, on the couch in the front of the store. Roseanne Barr popped in one day to buy makeup. I'd actually done her makeup many years before, when she was just breaking into the business. By the time she came to the studio, she was a full-blown star and was on a mission to buy, buy, buy. Susan Sarandon came in because she had forgotten her makeup bag while traveling and needed a few basics to get her through her stay in Los Angeles. I remember her as being very easy to work with, a nice woman, no fuss. The complete opposite was Joan Collins. She was looking for some very specific colors. She knew exactly what she wanted and purchased a couple of items. Before she left, I mentioned that some of my friends felt that I looked a lot like her sister, Jackie. She gave me a haughty once-over and said, "You don't look anything like her," and stomped out of the salon. I was so embarrassed!

Another regular at the Bobbe Joy Makeup Studio was fitness guru Jillian Michaels, who went on to star in *The Biggest Loser*. She was super bubbly, with an outgoing personality, and she was always willing to share workout tips with anyone in the store. Television newswoman Michaela Pereira was also a regular eyebrow client. She inspired me to work hard, have fun, and accept myself, which is her own very special mantra.

Many years earlier I had worked with Jane Seymour, but we had lost touch. Then one day, my son, Ian, was working with actor/director Stacy Keach, who was married to Jane, and they were going to have a Fourth of July party at their house at the beach. Ian mentioned to Stacy that his mom used to work with Jane and he had once gone to their house. Stacy said, "Why don't you invite your parents to the party?" We went, and I brought her some makeup as a gift. She was excited and happy to see me and loved the makeup. It was a wonderful reunion, and a few months later she came into the studio and reordered some of the makeup I'd given her. The studio gave me an opportunity to reconnect with old friends.

After a few months in the Bobbe Joy Makeup Studio, I knew that my timing had been perfect. I had tapped into a ready market. It was an era when women would get their makeup and hair done just to go out to dinner. I was able to give my clients that something special that kept them coming back. It was extremely gratifying, and I would have been happy for it to go on forever. But as I have learned, change is inevitable: no matter how well things are going, the world keeps turning. After about ten years I began to see the signs of what was coming next.

The big change started when MAC Cosmetics came into the picture. MAC was part of an already well-established franchise in Canada, developed by Frank Toskan, a makeup artist/photographer who had come up against the same limitations I had experienced. The popular brands of makeup did not look particularly good in photographs. Like me, he created a product he knew could work better on camera and would accommodate a wide range of skin types and colors. His advantage was that he worked with a business partner, Frank Angelo, who was able to take their "kitchen product" into a worldwide market.

When MAC Cosmetics arrived in the United States, it was the first makeup-buying experience that was free-standing and wasn't part of a larger store. The company didn't offer any makeup services, only products. It originally catered to the professional makeup artist, but soon the models wanted the MAC products not only for themselves but also for their friends and family members. It became known as the place where everybody went.

In order to compete, the department stores started hiring makeup artists to work at their cosmetic counters to do a "free makeup" along with a purchase. The licensing of beauticians was something that Aida Gray and I and a couple of other people had worked on in the 1970s. We were trying to get people licensed who did makeup profession- ally. Back then, you were either a cosmetologist, which meant you did everything related to hair and nails but mostly skin care and beauty treatments, or you were a manicurist. Then a new category of skin professional came into the picture—aesthetician, meaning someone who did only makeup and waxing and facials. In 1978 we finally got the licensing laws passed. The department store makeup artists didn't have licenses, and they couldn't charge for their services, but they could provide them for free as a way to introduce customers to their beauty products. It became a very popular promotional tool.

Suddenly, clients were coming to us saying, "I can buy a lipstick and get my makeup done for nothing." That really hurt business for the professional makeup artists and especially for those of us who were doing large groups, such as wedding parties. I remember a time when I was doing the makeup for a bunch of girls from Beverly Hills High School for their prom and the mother of one of the girls called and said, "She's changed her mind. She's going to go to the department store to get her makeup done."

That afternoon the mother called in a panic because evidently whatever they'd used on her daughter made her break out in a rash. I said, "Bring her in now." I put cold compresses all over her face and made her sit until the very last minute. I took off all her makeup and did it all over again. Fortunately, she was able to go to the prom. Her relieved mother thanked me profusely, and as she escorted her now happy daughter out of the studio, all I could think was, "Well, you get what you pay for."

With the mass marketing of MAC and the department stores handing out free makeups, icons like Aida Gray and Georgette Klinger were going out of business, and I could see the writing on the wall. Instead of folding my tent, I decided to unburden myself of a large storefront, employees, and overhead and rent a space in a salon where I was familiar with all the hairstylists and where a lot of my clients went. The shop was the Nelson J Salon in the heart of Beverly Hills.

I hired an assistant, brought all my makeup over, and was able to increase my net profits by decreasing my overhead and working one-on-one with my fabulous clients. Nelson's was a high-class salon where I could continue to service my clients and sell my products. I did that successfully for another six years, which along with my fourteen years at the Bobbe Joy Makeup Studio comprised my final twenty-year stretch in the makeup business. When I stopped production on my entire line of cosmetics, I left behind a lot of very unhappy customers who could no longer avail themselves of the Bobbe Joy Makeup Studio products.

In January 2018 I was truly ready to retire, or maybe I was just ready to stop working. The word "retirement" doesn't quite seem to fit me. I said I would know when the time had come for me to leave the business, and it was true. I left with no regrets. I am happy to have loved my work and to have been able to touch so many lives. Most importantly, my experiences and my incredible clients have left me with a heart full of pride and happiness. And lots of stories, too.

Promotional piece for Bobbe Joy Makeup Studio on South Beverly Drive in Beverly Hills

A sliver of the inside of Bobbe Joy Makeup Studio, with display cases

Photographer Harry Langdon Jr. and me at the opening of Bobbe Joy Makeup Studio, 1999

Collage of magazine covers and ads for Bobbe Joy Makeup Studio. We earned a lot of kudos!

156

Mitch and me walking our beautiful daughter, Portia, down the aisle for her wedding at Greystone Mansion, 2001

Me walking Ian down the aisle for his wedding at the Beverly Hills Hotel, 2002. Mitch was the officiant for the ceremony.

157

18

WORKING WITH MAKEUP

Nothing makes a woman more beautiful than the belief that she is beautiful.

—SOPHIA LOREN

As the years went by, the beauty industry grew, and companies became more receptive to creating private-label products for small businesses. Salon owners in Small Town, USA, began to create their own line of cosmetics. And in recent years we have seen another huge shift in the way cosmetics are marketed: we can buy everything through the internet without ever leaving home.

The downside is that anyone who thinks they know anything about makeup can create a video on YouTube and tell you how they put their makeup on. They just erase the face; slap on loads of foundation, concealer, and heavy powder; and then paint in the details. Most often the makeup is overdone and not at all what the majority of women can relate to. I've read a lot of stupid things in beauty magazines, too. The magazines derive most of their revenue from advertisers, who are mainly cosmetics manufactures. A lot of what they put in beauty magazines is to showcase what's going on in the world of makeup this year and on what's being promoted by the manufacturers. If yellow eye shadow and peach and green are on the menu, they're going to try to sell that to the public. I'm going to be the first person to say, "Please don't buy that. Please don't wear that." Nobody looks good in yellow eye shadow except the model on the cover who's been retouched within an inch of her life.

It's the same thing in fashion: if the fashion is short skirts now, it's going to be long skirts next year. Skinny pants? It will be flared pants next year. All the crap you bought will be out, and you'll have to buy new. And that's how it is with makeup. I would tell my clients, "You want to be fashionable? We can do it in a small way. We can use one thing and make that the happening thing." (Except if you're a young girl. Young girls can wear anything, except tons of black.) I subscribe to the "less is more" school of makeup, with the exception of special occasions, which may call for something a bit more elaborate.

Creating personalized makeup for specific clients was a joy, but it was very time-consuming and labor intensive. I am proud and happy to have been able to help so many people solve so many problems over the years, simply by creating and/or selecting the right colors for them.

Working at the Jon Peters Salon for so many years gave me a solid foundation for the twenty years I spent working in television, film, print, commercials, and videos. What I needed to learn for the film and TV world was how to work fast, read scripts, and understand how to create looks for specific characters. One of the most important elements I learned about was lighting. In my new profession, lighting, texture, and color were all crucial components, and each one had to be controlled to make the client look flawless. When I was working on salon customers, I had no control over the lighting in their everyday lives.

In still photography, retouching was a specific art and could make anyone look picture-perfect. And now we can photograph ourselves with our digital phones and change whatever we don't like about ourselves before we post it or send it to our friends. However, we can't retouch ourselves in the real world; that's when we need a professional to advise us on how much or how little makeup we should apply to present ourselves to the world. As we move through our day in offices, restaurants, stores, schools, daytime, nighttime—whenever, wherever—we must find colors, textures, and techniques to help us keep looking our best.

By the time I retired from the film and television world and opened the Bobbe Joy Makeup Studio, I had years of experience behind me and plenty of time to think about the specifics of what I had learned over those past twenty years. Especially, I looked back on the lessons I learned that could be helpful to the average woman, who wasn't seeking the calculated perfection of the movie screen but who wanted to use her own natural looks to her best advantage.

That's when the average woman needs help from a professional makeup artist, not a salesperson trying to push the latest lime-green eye shadow. My recommendation is to invest in a lesson or two from a professional makeup artist and you'll be on your way to understanding what is best for YOU.

If you live in an urban area, you most likely will be able to find a professional makeup artist who can guide you to what works best for your skin color, age, facial structure, and hair color. *Allure* magazine has been doing a "Best of" series all over the United States for many years. Chances are they have been to an area near you. Look up who they recommend in the city closest to you. (We were named Best Makeup Lessons in Beverly Hills.) In case you live far away from that kind of one-on-one advice, then here are some of the "dos and don'ts" that can help you when you think about doing your own makeup. It can all be done beautifully and efficiently, with just a few additions or subtractions.

(I promise not to make this sound like a graduate course! It's relatively simple.)

I do a very clean makeup. I like it when you look at yourself and you don't see one particular feature; you see the overall face. "I'm not going to make you look like a hooker" was my standard line, and the thing I say to women all the time is "if you want to look natural or pretty, keep your makeup within a certain color tone, and it will always look natural." (I'll explain more about color tones later.)

There are no cookie-cutter rules or we wouldn't have so many choices. However, we can usually dismiss a large swath of items, because, for example, if you're not under twenty-five, most of the crazy innovations are not for you—unless you want to look like a cartoon character. Also, the soft light of the evening can be extremely flattering, but if you step into a harsher light, you could end up looking like a painted doll if you put on too much makeup or if it's too dark for your complexion or hair color.

It's like choosing the right wardrobe for wherever you're going, whether it's the office, a dinner date, a special occasion, a vacation, or just running errands. I wouldn't be seen dead in a dress cut down to "there" or up to "where"! Purple and orange may look great in the Caribbean but could fail miserably in the office. Smoky eyes might be fabulous for a night on the town but would look ridiculous on a Caribbean beach. And I know not to wear electric-blue eye shadow—ever!—even if it's the hottest color on the runway.

UNDERSTANDING COLOR: Most people are attracted to certain colors, and although I'm not a big fan of defining oneself as a "season,"

I do think that certain colors look better on certain people. You need to know what's best for you and make it your own. So how do you know what to buy? Here are a few color rules (and, remember, rules are meant to be broken!):

First, you need to assess your skin, hair, and eyes: are they warm or cool?

SKIN

WARM TONES: If you are a warm tone, you have some pink in your skin. You might be fair, have rosacea, or have olive or dark skin with undertones of pink, red, or gold.

If your skin has a warm tone, then these are the best colors for you: peach, bronze, gold, copper, warm brown, orangey pink, orange red, yellow, cream, rose gold, turquoise, browny rose—and, of course, black.

COOL TONES: Cool tone skin colors can range from very pale beige, to olive with yellow to dark ashy, to plain brown.

If your skin has a cool tone, you'll look best in pink, purple, khaki, navy, gray, cool brown, blue, red, white, silver—and, of course, black.

HAIR

WARM HAIR COLORS include blonde, red, and brunette, with red or golden undertones.

COOL HAIR COLORS are blonde, brunette, gray, and black, with the absence of any red or gold.

EYES

Blue-eyed people look great in peach tones, blue gray, and bronze, while green-eyed people look great in rose, gold, and purple. Brown-eyed look good in almost anything, depending on whether they have a warm or cool skin tone.

Next you need to decide on your color palette. Here are some tips to help you find your best shades:

1. Think realistically about your age.

As we get older, our skin and hair lose their color and can lack shine, and we can look pale. We NEED some color, either in our clothing or in our makeup—or both—to uplift us. But some color is good at any age.

2. What color attracts you, and which tone is best for you?

Some of it is fashion, some is psychological, and sometimes color just makes us happy or reflects our mood. We often read blanket advice in magazines like: "After fifty you should only wear red lipstick." Well that's a lot of BS, because some people don't look good in red lipstick at any age. Wearing certain colors of red lipstick also requires that you look at the color of your teeth. If they appear to be tinged yellow, then it is important to select a red lipstick with blue undertones to counteract the yellow. If your teeth are bright white, then a true red can be worn.

I cannot wear a bright true red. I tried it, and everybody laughed at me. They were like, "Oh my God, you look awful!" But in the evening for an event when I'm dressed up and I want the defining something on my lips, I'll do something like a deep plum, and since I'm a warm-toned person, I will accent the lipstick with a gold gloss to make it softer, so it's not as jarring!

On the other hand, I have a client who is the epitome of red lipstick. Her coloring is dark with dark hair. Short and spiky, really hip. Beautiful clothes, beautiful jewelry: all of that and she puts that red lipstick on, and it's like "Wow!" She doesn't need anything else. As a rule, a lot of Asian women look great in red lipstick as well. Skin tone is part of it, and you can keep their eyes soft and their brows strong, with a beautiful red lip. But for certain women who have silver hair or maybe dark brown with silver in it, red lipstick can be jarring on them, so you have to have something to balance it. Most often, a little blush and a drop of gloss to highlight the red lipstick is all you need. (You just can't take a lady off the street, put red lipstick on her, and say, "Wow, she looks great.")

It's important to note that anyone who chooses to wear red lipstick must follow these suggestions: 1. Lips must be in perfect condition. Scrub dry skin and moisturize to ensure that you have a clean surface. 2. Using a mirror, prime and line your lips with the appropriate lip pencil (in a color close to your lipstick). 3. Then apply lipstick (with a lip brush, especially if your lips are a bit on the thinner side) very carefully, staying inside the lip liner. Note: There is nothing attractive about smudged red lipstick either sticking to chapped lips or bleeding into cracks and crevices outside the lip liner.

3.   Where and how you live affect your taste.

Cold weather usually produces darker, drabber colors, and as spring appears, color comes out to play, and so do we. Those of us who live in warmer climates usually have the pick of whatever the fashion world is promoting at the time. It's fun to stay in tune with the changing seasons; just make sure that you find the version of what's being promoted that is right for you.

4. What's your taste?

If you're a fashionista and pink is the color of the moment, then pink it is—hot pink, fuchsia pink, baby pink, rose, magenta, all of them—and just like the models in the magazines, you'll want your makeup to work perfectly with whatever the latest color is. This is how we amass a drawer full of makeup, most of which never gets used past one season.

As you go from decade to decade, you'll find that your tastes change and a color that appealed to you all through your twenties may not appeal to you in your forties. When you do your annual closet clean-out, that might also be a good time to take a look at your makeup collection and get rid of that orange eye shadow that once looked great, but not anymore, or that old favorite lipstick that's so dry it sticks to your lips.

The best part of all this is that you can always shop for some new product. And when you do, stop and think about my advice to my clients: "Don't buy that; you already have three of those!" and "Why would you choose that? The color's all wrong for you."

How many lipsticks, eye shadows, pencils, etc., is it realistic to have? This question is the same as "How many pairs of shoes should you have in your closet?" You should have enough so you don't get bored and not so many they sit in your drawer and never get used.

When you do go shopping for makeup, make sure you keep my nagging voice in your head so you won't keep buying the same items over and over that you NEVER, EVER wear!

5. What about transitioning your makeup from one season to the next?

In the warmer months you probably will want to keep your face makeup light, especially if you live in a very warm climate. Sometimes just using a self-tanning cream is enough to give you a healthy bit of color. Bronzers also are perfect for the warmer months. You can use them on your cheeks, forehead, and chin and over your eyelids to warm up your skin tone. They come in all shades, so you have lots of choices.

Usually, cooler months mean darker wardrobe colors, so you will want to adjust your lip color to go with a plum, red, navy, brown, or gray as opposed to softer, lighter pastels that work in warmer months. It's the same for eye shadow colors. If you are wearing a turquoise blouse, you are probably not going to wear dark smoky eyes. You don't need to match your eye makeup to that turquoise; however, you might choose a soft brown, rose, peach, or soft gray to enhance the look.

* * *

How you put your makeup on is also of great importance. A complete makeup session is included in the final chapter, but here are a few basics you can start implementing right away.

Powder can be aging; it gets into the cracks and crevices and makes the skin look dry. So after forty, keep it to a minimum.

Use a lip pencil to define the lip line and to keep lipstick from bleeding. Try to get your pencil color as close as possible to your lipstick color.

Add a little foundation to lighten or change lipstick color.

Use moisturizing tints or mineral tints to even out the skin.

Use stick concealer only on blemishes or dark spots, to maintain a natural look.

Curl your eyelashes. It's important to open your eyes wide to make them appear larger. If your doctor will provide you with a prescription, use Latisse. It helps strengthen, lengthen, and thicken your lashes.

Keep eye shadow color soft and understated, especially during the day.

Use liner to define and lift eyes, together with an eyelash curler and mascara.

Here's the big question: to line or not to line under the eye?

1. For very small eyes, don't line under the eye—just mascara.

2. For medium-sized eyes, line under, with a slightly lighter color than for the eyelid.

Some of the softer-color eyeliners include a blue gray, khaki, eggplant, chocolate, or ash brown. Example: Black or dark brown on the top lid and a softer brown under the bottom lashes.

For large eyes you may line on both the top and bottom; however, if your eyes are close together, concentrate the liner from the center of the eye to the outer corners and slightly beyond, to give the illusion of elongating the eye. I generally prefer that the lower liner just be drawn from the center of the lower lashes to the outer corner of the eyes, while the upper liner can start from the top inside corner of the eye.

• • •

Once you understand these basic tricks, you can start practicing and experimenting on your own. Try different colors of eye shadow to see what makes your eyes pop and different kinds of eyeliners to see which kind works best for you. Products react differently on various skin types, and you need to discover which ones suit you best. This is where going into one of the new mega makeup stores or department stores can work to your advantage. Try the testers liberally. Just be sure they have been cleaned properly and use the throwaway applicators. You'll know right away whether something feels good, and with a little practice you'll begin to know whether it looks good.

19

EYEBROWS, LIFTS, AND PLASTIC SURGERY

Don't set yourself on fire in order to keep others warm.

—BRIAN LEE SLAVIN

Twenty years ago we were shaping eyebrows, long before it became wildly popular. It was one of my specialties both at Jon Peters and at the Bobbe Joy Makeup Studio. As a result, I have some strong opinions about some of the terrible things people do to their eyebrows, mostly because they want to be trendy. I've said it a million times and will say it again, "Eyebrows are not a fashion statement."

When you're a child, you have full eyebrows. As you get older, you start tweezing the hairs, trying to create a clean line, and, slowly but surely, you find yourself tweezing out more and more. "Oh, maybe I'll take that one, and now that I did, this one doesn't look so good." And before you know it, you don't have any eyebrows. I recommend penciling a line before you tweeze. That way, when you take the pencil off, you still have an eyebrow. You have to protect those brows, because a lot of times, as you get older, the hairs don't grow back.

When the Kardashians made thick eyebrows their signature, everyone wanted to copy them. I get it. I was always telling people, "Please don't make your eyebrows thin, because it's aging." The thicker your eyebrow, the more youthful you look. I kept a lot of women from overplucking and thinning their eyebrows, and those women were very happy when the thick eyebrow trend caught on. But it isn't for everyone. You have to look at an individual's face. Someone with a small face and small eyes is not going to look attractive with a bushy eyebrow. There has to be a balance on their face. If it looks right, your eyebrows won't be walking in the door before you do.

Then there's the case of girls and women who bleach their hair blonde, with blown-up lips, big boobs, anorexic bodies, and big, thick black eyebrows. There are models who wear that look, but it's like wearing yellow eye shadow; it's not for the average woman walking down the street. That's a fashion victim, and it's just mindboggling to me that women don't realize how unattractive that look is on them. It's not pretty or soft or sexy. They just see something they think looks good on someone else and say, "I want that, and I want that," and it's like saying, "I want a sky-bluepink outfit." You're not coordinating yourself properly. I want to say to them, "Do you look in the mirror?"

There are other women who have quite a different attitude about makeup. That's the woman who gets facials and works out and grooms her eyebrows but doesn't want to do anything with makeup. When I see that woman, I say to myself, "There's someone I can work with, because she cares about how she looks." The difficult women are those who don't care at all. I understand if you're busy, but you can at least take five minutes to think about how you present yourself.

When I'm talking to women who have no fashion or beauty sense, I can only supply the cheerleading part of it and give them ideas. For these women it goes beyond their makeup. Some of them have no idea about the simple basics of putting together their wardrobe. I try my best to give them a little shove in the right direction. I can show them pictures of how to coordinate these pants with that shirt. If I'm wearing full pants, I'm not going to wear a big, giant shirt over my full pants at my height. I have a petite frame. I can't carry all that fabric. It would swallow me up. If you wear a big bottom, wear a smaller top. If you're going to wear a big top, wear a smaller bottom. That's how it works. It's very easy, and it's knowing what works for your body. My mom was very big on top, very big busted and wide, but she had skinny little legs, so she always wore thinner pants and a fuller top, and it looked good. And it wasn't that she was a fashionista, but she understood the principle of proportion and what complemented her figure.

Knowing yourself goes further than just wardrobe, hair, and makeup. What is your lifestyle? How much time are you willing to put into making yourself look the way you want? Are you so busy that you don't think you have time to do it? I know women have busy lives, especially if they work and/or raise children.

My girlfriend Gayle, may she rest in peace, always said, "You can't make a dog a horse." You can change women's thinking, but you can't make them do what they don't want to do. If you get up in the morning and you're happy with the way you look and you're not going to put lipstick on—even though I say that if you just put lipstick on, it will brighten your face—then that would be it. When I opened the Bobbe Joy Makeup Studio, I understood that whatever I did, I needed to make my recommendations work for the clients and be sure that they were easy and manageable and fit their lifestyle.

Over the years I developed the skills to work with almost every type of client. First of all, I have to know whom I'm dealing with before I start. If somebody comes in and says to me, "I want to look like you," I say, "I can't make you look like me. But I can make you look like the best you that you can be, and we can take all of these ideas and work together to make that happen. But you're not going to look like me. You have red hair; I have whatever color. You have small eyes; I have big eyes. You have thin eyebrows; I have thick eyebrows. What I give you will suit you. It's going to be your look. It's not going to be mine or anyone else's."

After fifty-one years of talking to women, it's absolutely fascinating what women will do to themselves, or what they think they need to do to themselves, in order to make themselves feel good. And that's really what it's all about in the end. When we think we look good, we feel good. Any woman who's looked in the mirror and pulled her cheeks back or lifted her eyelids knows how seductive it is to think we can turn back time with a few little tricks.

One of my favorite tricks was taught to me early on when I was doing Stockard Channing's makeup and she asked me whether I'd ever done lifts. I said, "No, I know about them, but I've never done them," and she said, "Well, I like to use them. Can I show you how to do it?" I said, "Absolutely," and she taught me one of the great Hollywood beauty secrets, how to do "lifts." This was not a surgical procedure; this was a little bit of true Hollywood magic.

Let's say your neck or jowls are starting to sag. There are little squares of tape that you put by the upper portion of your ear; the tape is connected to a little string. The string is attached to a clip, and you take this string and clip it under your hair, toward the back of your head, and you pull the clip down while you pull the string up. That pulls up your face and holds it in place. Sometimes you have to make a pin curl to hook it to, and a lot of women who did that wore wigs over them. And if you wanted to do your neck, you'd place the tape just behind the lower portion of the ear and clip it up higher on your head. It was pretty cool. And then to hide the tape, you take a little bit of spirit gum and dab it onto the tape, and then you take the little hairs that are right by the side of your face and you press them into the spirit gum so it looks like your hair is there. And that's it.

A lot of stars use this technique for film, especially when the character has to age during the story. They'll use "lifts" when they want the character to be younger, and then as they get older, they just drop everything and add more makeup to make them look older. That was Hollywood's instant answer to sagging skin, but it has nothing to do with what is commonly known as a face-lift—that's plastic surgery. Practically speaking, "lifts" are for stage, screen, and TV.

This whole surgical thing, whether they want the Ivanka Trump look or whether it's these women who think that the bigger their lips are, the bigger their boobs are, the higher their cheekbones are, all of that stuff—making them all look like stamped-out versions of the Housewives of Wherever—is absurd. And what's more absurd is the doctors who are offering these surgeries.

A client would come in and say, "I'm thinking about having my lips done."

I'd say, "How do you want to do it?"

They'd say, "I like the poufy look."

I'd say, "Really? The kind that looks like you're sucking a golf ball through a garden hose? What is it you like about it?"

"Well, it's sexy."

"Really? And what kind of man do you think is going to be attracted to you when you look like that? Someone who wants an arm piece but not somebody who wants to have a real relationship. If you want to do it, go do it, but just know that that's where your life is going to go."

Some women would say, "I'm thinking about going to Doctor So-and-So," and I'd say, "Why don't you get a second opinion?" You could do that back in the days before doctors charged at least $500 for a consultation to discourage women who were "window-shopping." It's a whole different ball game now. I always say, "Really look at the people who have had surgery done before you do it." I mean, see whether they're happy with the outcome and what you think of the results. Some of these doctors play God and really think they know what is good for the patient. Some of them do what the women want because they figure if they don't do it, another doctor is going to do it, so they might as well make the money. A lot of them aren't really "doing no harm," as they say in the medical profession. I have always opted for doctors who just wanted to make you look refreshed. Clean you up a bit. That's it. The rest of it is mentally unhealthy to me. I really cannot look at these women with these giant cheekbone implants that are pushed up so far they're burying their eyes.

There are plastic surgeons performing procedures on women (and men) that they shouldn't be doing, in order to chase the holy grail of youth and beauty. We've seen what's been done to some popular actresses, like blowing up their lips to be so unnatural they look ridiculous. The big problem, if you are an actor, is that it puts you into a different category; you've changed your look, and you no longer can be what it is that made you unique and interesting in front of the camera. A bad surgery can mark the end of your career. I fault the doctors for that.

Some actors, like Jane Fonda, have had remarkable results, but there are too many others whose careers have been ruined by bad plastic surgery. There is something about being who you are. You can't be Judi Dench or Meryl Streep when you're older if you've had all that extensive plastic surgery. So you have to choose what kind of an actor you want to be. What kind of a person in society do you want to be, and how do you want people to see you?

The thing you should strive for is to refresh yourself or clean yourself up. That's what I call it. What these doctors do is pull too tight. You can see pleats sometimes on the sides of the patient's face. You can see that they're so pulled that their smile lines, instead of being natural, are angled out on the side. You know? Because they're lifting it up. The other thing is putting in cheek implants that are too large for their face. Doctors tell their patients, "I can lift your face up by putting these cheek implants in." Now there are people who do beautiful cheek implants and are smart enough to know that you lose some filling in your lips. They do just the lip line to define it, to make it look like it's more than it is, but not to go over it or lift up your lips.

I'm going to tell a story about plastic surgery that I think is important. I admit that I had a face-lift. I was fifty-eight, and I had a face-lift. Before I did, one of my clients who worked for a plastic surgeon here in Beverly Hills suggested that he and I meet because maybe we could send each other clients. Now, that's never been my thing. I only like to recommend people whom I've had personal experience with. But I said OK because he was a doctor who had been on one of those plastic surgery makeover shows. I went to lunch with him. We're sitting there talking, and I said to him, "I'm thinking of having my face done."

I already had an appointment with my plastic surgeon, who was a doctor I highly recommend to others.

I asked him, "What would you do?"

He said, "Well, the first thing I would do is give you a mid-face-lift, where they take the fat from your jawline and move it up into your cheeks."

"So you look like you have chipmunk cheeks," I thought.

"Number two, I would give you a brow lift."

I thought, "Where is he going to lift my brows? Doesn't he see how high my brows already are?"

"And the third thing I would do is give you an upper lip lift, because it makes you look younger when you can see your upper teeth."

Fast forward, I couldn't wait to get out of there. What I wanted to say to him was, "You obviously don't think I'm very attractive, because you want to change my face to look like someone I'm not." But I didn't, because I wasn't ballsy enough then. But that's what I tell women now. I always advise that if somebody's going to try to change your face and do weird things, you need to tell them no right then and there and leave.

A couple of weeks after meeting with the plastic surgeon who wanted to trade referrals with me, I had my face done. Two weeks later I was back in my store on South Beverly Drive doing a client's makeup. Next to me one of my assistants was working on another client, and I heard her say to the client, "Did you have a face-lift?"

She said, "Yeah, I just did."

I said, "That's interesting; I just did, too."

I wasn't going to hide it. But I looked at her, and this is what I saw: this upper lip lift with her front teeth prominently exposed like Bucky Beaver. And I said, "Oh, did Dr. So-and-So do you?"

She said, "Yes, how did you know?"

I said, "He's really popular right now."

I thought to myself, "There but for the grace of God go I." It could have been me sitting there had I not been smart enough to know better. I'm very outspoken about plastic surgery and how I feel about it. If you want to look better and if you want to look ten years younger and you feel comfortable doing it, do it. If you don't feel comfortable, don't do it. Own it. Whatever it is, own it. I'm owning my hanging neck. I'm not liking it, but I'm owning it. I don't know how women feel in Middle America, but I know how it is on either coast: it's scary. You walk down the street, and it's frightening to see what women are allowing their plastic surgeons to do to them.

Some of the guidelines I would recommend for women contemplating plastic surgery are, first of all, look at before and after pictures of patients. If you know somebody who has had it done and you can look at them and see they still look like themselves, that's one way. You should also have at least two consultations; unfortunately, it costs a lot of money to go to these doctors now, but you need at least two consultations. Three would be better. And listen carefully to what they're telling you. Ask a lot of questions. It's very important that you ask: Am I going to look pulled? Am I going to still look like myself? Are my eyes going to look surprised? You should expect a face-lift to last eight to ten years. Mine's lasted a long time, sixteen years. That's damn good.

I don't believe that you should do it when you're thirty. That's ridiculous—almost as bad is people getting Botox injections early (even in their twenties) because they think it's going to prevent them from having wrinkles later in life. I don't like Botox parties, where health practitioners give it away like vitamins. Some people swear by these nurse practitioners who do it; very possibly they're very good, but there are definite risks. You don't want to hit a blood vessel. I think if you're going to do Botox, it should be done appropriately, by someone who really knows what they're doing. I have gone only to an aesthetic dermatologist who has administered Botox for years. I just feel more comfortable with a doctor. People go to nurses because it's cheaper. It's like anything else. People went to South America and had plastic surgery because it was cheaper, and then they wound up with big problems. So you know you have to weigh the risks and you have to decide how important this is to you. How important is it to your life? Remember I was in the beauty business, so for me it was important that I maintained a certain standard, but I wanted to help women look beautiful without plastic surgery if they were against it. Going under the knife is not for everyone, and it can lead to medical complications if not done correctly, to say nothing of disfiguring a woman. My goal as a makeup artist was to help women look and feel their best.

European women, in general, have a better handle on the aging process. Nobody ever told them it was terrible to get old. I think that we've just been told so many horrible things. We've been told somehow that after the age of thirty-five, we're not hot anymore. It's like we don't have a mind of our own, everybody telling us what we should and shouldn't think, and we've been told so many lies about how we should be and not be. I find it offensive. Let's say, for example, you have a woman who is really pretty and has been pretty her whole life. Now she looks in the mirror, and she doesn't see pretty anymore. She sees old. She's still pretty by other people's standards. But she doesn't believe she's pretty because she hasn't accepted the aging process. You have to like yourself enough to let go of unrealistic standards.

There are many beautiful older women. Why? Because they believe they are. If you don't believe you are, you don't put that out there, and then you are what you think you are. I mean it's been hard for me, but I'll tell you that it wasn't until I saw the documentary on Iris Apfel, the interior designer and stylist, that some of this made sense to me. I think she's so fabulous. She looks so fabulous, and she puts herself together without rules and regulations. She is who she is, even at age ninety-eight. She is an inspiration. She is her own unique creation from top to bottom. Just take a look at her fabulous glasses, her haircut, her makeup, her smile—it all works. Her style has evolved throughout her life, and she has the confidence to pick and choose what looks good on her. She is her own artistic creation!

In your mind's eye, you need to have an idea of how you want to look or how you want to be seen. Go online or read magazines and just take a look at ideas. And if you can afford to, why not hire somebody to help you shop so you feel good? So that's what I'm trying to get at. Go out there and experiment and buy something new and different. You don't have to spend a lot of money.

Women who totally and completely give up, I have no respect for them. I don't care how evolved you are. There is something to be said for taking care of yourself and living a good life, and if you just think you can allow yourself to be invisible, I think that's a very sad state.

My friend Marion Rosenberg, a well-known Hollywood manager and producer, is a beautiful and energetic woman in her early eighties. I loved what she said when someone asked her, "What did you do?" and Marion quickly replied, "What do you mean, 'What *did* I do?' I'm still doing it." She's still working in her eighties and finding fulfillment through her career and is excited about life. It's contagious!

Those are choices you make. If you're lucky enough to have your health, the world is your oyster, and you can create whatever kind of life you want, whatever image fits you, and whatever happiness you can discover. It will be written all over your face.

My choice was to retire because I wanted to see what else life had to offer, not because I wanted to curl up in a ball and die.

20

EYELASHES AND SKIN CARE

*There is nothing more rare, nor more beautiful,
than a woman being unapologetically herself;
comfortable in her perfect imperfection.
To me, that is the true essence of beauty.*

—STEVE MARIBOLI

By now you can see that every feature of your face has its own challenges, and each one needs to be addressed in its own way. Take eyelashes, for instance: many women try to solve their eyelash issues with a set of false lashes, which they take out of the box and stick on. Rarely does that work, but people do it because they don't know any different. If you came to me, I would cut the eyelashes to fit your eye shape and glue them just above the lash line so that they would look like your lashes, only thicker, wispier, and better. They would be tailored to fit your face.

Back in the days of the Jon Peters Salon, I recognized that what was being offered on the market was not up to my standards, and I decided to create my own eyelashes and customize them for my clients. This was very time-consuming, involving an apparatus my father built for me that held a taut fishing line to which we would hand tie individual hairs. You took a hair, and you did a slip knot with it. We'd do them long, and there was a glue that we would apply at the end just to keep the ends from falling off. Then I would trim them to a decent length. I fashioned a wooden dowel around which I would wrap the lashes and then adhere them with the hair-setting solution DEP and a little water. After they dried, I would remove them from the dowel and proceed to cut and customize them for my clients. Today, I would do it differently, but back then we didn't know. Nowadays, lashes come in all shapes and sizes, although they still should be cut for each individual person.

If the false eyelashes were curled, you had to curl your own eyelashes, because once you put them on, you would want them to hold up the other lashes. Also, when looking at a person wearing lashes, if their own lashes were not curled, you would be able to see the separation between the false lashes and their own, and that is not a pretty look.

My whole theory on eyelash curlers is that if you want to look awake and alive and have big eyes, use an eyelash curler. Curl your own lashes, put mascara on, then put the false eyelashes on. They should all blend together without your own lashes sticking out straight from the curled false lashes.

If someone came in and didn't have big eyes, we would trim the false eyelashes to fit their face. I also did individual lashes too. They were not individually one on ones but little clumpy ones where you just curl the lashes, put on mascara, and set them between your own lashes so it looks like you have more lashes. Depending on how you slept determined how long they'd last. For some people it was just an evening. Other people slept like they were dead, and they could hold on to the false lashes for a week.

That was another thing I learned: when a woman comes in and has expensive makeup done, she is loath to take it off at night. Maybe she went to a wedding that night, and the next day there was a breakfast or a party or something and she wants to keep the makeup on. I'm not a big proponent of sleeping in your makeup, but I understood the dilemma, and sometimes I would say to them, "Why don't you do this? Take your makeup off from your eyes down. Foundation and everything off. Take a cotton swab and clean around your eyes. Go to sleep and leave your eye makeup on. In the morning, put your moisturizer back on, put your face makeup back on and blush, and just fix whatever looks messy." This is just for special occasions, certainly not for every night.

You don't want to sleep with your face makeup on because it gets into your pores. Not only that, but it doesn't look good the next day. Also, it's not healthy for your skin. You need your skin to breathe. My theory has always been there has to be a time when your skin breathes. I don't wear anything on my face at night. This has been my theory all these years. I literally do not wear any cream at night. Sometimes if I feel I'm really dry in the winter, I'll put cream under my eyes and around my mouth. But I want my skin to breathe. I don't know whether that's something the dermatologist would think is a good idea or not. It's just my idea, and it works for me. Besides, I save a lot of money not having to buy expensive night creams.

The most important thing is keeping your skin clean. I'm not a skin specialist, but I can talk about removing makeup. You have to take it off. Don't sleep in your makeup. As far as getting your makeup off, I like to use a makeup wipe first, and then I wash my face with either a cleanser or a light soap. I also use a wet washcloth and lightly scrub until the washcloth comes away totally clean. I like to use a microderm scrub on my skin at least once or twice a week (that's a cream that has microbeads in it). I just massage it in, and then I take a washcloth and wash it off. It's good for your skin because it takes off the outer layer of dead skin.

Because I have my own skin care routine, I haven't promoted facials a lot. However, I do see the benefits of cleaning and massaging. As you get older, your skin tends to dry out, and facials can stimulate collagen, which fights the aging process.

I think that you have to use eye makeup remover. I love the makeup wipes, but they don't get everything, and they can't take off mascara. So there's only a couple of ways to go. One is eye makeup remover, and there are some that are really good. The other option is soap and water. That will get it completely off. So that's what I do. There are many different products for removing makeup, but I'm not into trying nine million things. Just find the one that works with your skin.

I don't really want to tell you that I sleep in my mascara every night, but it's true. Despite everything I just said, I sleep in my mascara. I have very long lashes, and I wear a lot of mascara, and it's a pain to take it off. All the rest of my eye makeup and face makeup is removed. If I rub my eyes when I sleep, when I get up in the morning, some of the mascara has flaked off, so I take a dry cotton swab and gently roll it around to clean up the flakes. I comb through my lashes, which removes most of the residue, and curl them again and put a little fresh mascara on them. I don't know whether I would tell everybody to do this, but it works for me, especially because I have such thick lashes.

My thick lashes are not accidental or a gift of nature. Long ago I discovered a product called Latisse, a liquid that actually grows your eyelashes long and thick. It's a prescription product that you can get from your dermatologist or ophthalmologist. As you can imagine, it's rather pricey. But I've discovered a secret that makes it a whole lot more reasonable to use. They're going to hate me at Latisse but . . .

When you buy Latisse, they give little brushes and tell you to put the liquid onto the brush and use one on each eye per day and throw the brush away, which means you'll get about thirty days' worth of product. An ophthalmologist's wife told me this: "Throw the brushes away or use them for something else. You waste so much of the stuff when you put it on a brush because it soaks it all up. Get a thin eyeliner brush and squeeze one drop on the back of your hand—literally one drop—and draw it on right at your top lash line like you're putting on eyeliner. Never on your bottom lashes because it could get into your eye. Whatever's left, put it on your eyebrows." Some people swear that it works on your brows as well. Never hurts to try. So that's how I do it. Just make sure you rinse and dry the brush every day.

Barbara Mandrell; Mitch; Barbara's husband, Ken Dudney; and me at the
ceremony of the rededication of their marriage in Nashville

My husband, Mitch, with Michaela Pereira, television
anchor, and me at the Beverly Hills Rotary Club

Mitch and me with fashionista Mr. Blackwell. He declared me the best-dressed woman at the event!

Tim Gunn and me at the opening of Nespresso in Beverly Hills, October 2013. Love him!

189

Dolly and me at the 2018 screening of Dumplin'

Barbara Mandrell, me, and Dick Van Dyke on the set of Diagnosis Murder, *1997*

21

HOW TO DO YOUR MAKEUP

At their dressing table every woman has a chance to be an artist, and "Art," as Aristotle said, "completes what nature left unfinished."

—SOPHIA LOREN

Women need to be given permission to like what they see when they look in the mirror. Unfortunately, the images we see on television or in magazines set us up for constant disappointment. We can't help comparing ourselves with the latest "hot" actress or model whose face takes up the entire page in *Vogue*. What we don't know is what we *need* to know: that when that actress or model began her day, she didn't look quite the way she appears in the magazine. The flawless impressions that we see and wish for are accomplished by lighting, camera angles, filters, fans, clothes pinned or fitted perfectly, professional makeup and hair people, and, in the end, digital enhancement.

Marketing experts tell us that if we have any imperfections—blemishes, age spots, wrinkles, gray hair, bulges or lack thereof—we are inferior and must immediately invest in one or all of their products to achieve perfection. And if we fail to do so, the entire male population will look elsewhere. The truth is that most men don't even notice the new dress we bought, let alone whether our left pinkie has a chipped nail, but we continue to be dissatisfied with most of what we see about ourselves.

It's my belief that feeling attractive contributes to a woman's self-esteem. It's my hope to re-educate her thinking on how to make the most of the beauty she already has. This can be achieved with little effort, a bit of education, lots of patience, and some practice at learning how to apply makeup quickly, efficiently, and creatively.

Let's get started!

1. CLEANSE

The critical first step is to start with a clean face. You can use cleansing wipes, liquid face cleanser, or a cream to remove all makeup. After cleansing, take a washcloth with just water and keep cleaning until there's no residue on the washcloth. What it also does is act as an exfoliator, which is great, because that way you're always sloughing off dead skin and you're not applying makeup on top of dead skin.

2. MOISTURIZE

Once you put your moisturizer on, let it sit for a couple of minutes just to let it soak in. Brush your teeth, brush your hair, or make your bed. Just let your moisturizer soak in and dry.

3. PRIMER

Use a silicone-based primer and let it dry. I use a silicone-based face primer because it's so smooth and helps affix your makeup. It fills in fine lines, makes pores less visible, and makes for a perfect canvas. Let it sit for a minute, just so you're not mixing your makeup into it, then apply your makeup on top of it.

4. FOUNDATION

Select a foundation based on how much coverage you want. I like to use either a light foundation or a mineral tint of some kind, because what you're doing is just evening out your complexion. You're not trying to use it as a cover up. (When buying foundation, be sure to step outside into the light with a mirror to make sure the color blends with your skin tone and there's no line of demarcation on your neck or jawline.)

When applying foundation, squeeze out a little bit of the makeup onto the back of one hand (and if you can't find just the right color, you might add a second color to get it perfect). I generally mix two different foundations together, because you may love one color, but it needs a little bit more pink or you need to lighten it a little bit. Mix the two colors on the back of your hand, and then, using the fingers of your other hand, pat and blend it all over your face. It's not a cover-up; it just smooths everything out. You don't have to have a lot of different brushes. I find that your hands are one of the best tools. Put it all over, including your eyelids, which tend to be red. (If necessary, add a stick foundation for more coverage.)

5. CONCEALER

I have two different concealers. First, I use the concealer that goes underneath the eye, because most of us have some dark shadows under our eyes. I like to use a liquid in a wand that has a lot of pigment in it, but it's still a

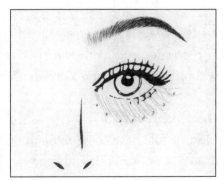

liquid—because if you use a cream, it's so thick that it gets into the cracks. All you do is dot it under your eyes, because you don't want too much. Choose one or two shades lighter than your foundation. Then take a foundation brush and just lightly spread it and blend it down. Start with a small amount, because you'd rather go back and put on more than have to worry about what to do with what you have left over. So you blend it under the eye and then up to your lash line, and then you blend it out and down.

6. STICK CONCEALER

Next you take your stick concealer, which is actually a foundation, because it contains more pigment and provides more coverage. (Try to find one as close to the color of your skin as possible. Most cosmetics lines make them in a wide variety of colors.) Using your fingers or a foundation brush, dot and blend the stick foundation wherever you have brown spots, red marks, or large pore areas. Using a foundation brush or your fingers, dot and blend until it's done its job. Most people use a brush, but I use my fingers. I like to put it on my nose where I have bigger pores because it fills in the pores a little bit. I also like to put a little over my eyelids to smooth out the color and prep for my eye shadow. Now it's a concealer that also acts as a base. (Just be sure you don't put it all over your face or you will look like you've been embalmed!)

7. POWDER

Use powder only if necessary. Use a soft translucent powder (one without any color) and a powder brush.

8. EYEBROWS

Most people have some difficulty with how to shape and fill in their brows. Your brows should generally look like two parallel lines on an angle to your highest point, which is your arch, and then an elongated triangle that indicates the tail of your brow.

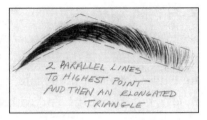

Begin your brow by using a pencil or a slim brush handle to line up the inside corner of your eye with the inside beginning of your brow. Draw a dot where you want your brow to start.

Now, looking straight into the mirror, place a second dot where the outside of your iris lines up with your arch. That will tell you where the highest portion of your arch should be.

Last, angle your pencil or handle from the edge of your nostril to the end of your eye upward. That will indicate just about where to end your brow. Place a third dot.

Starting from the first dot, lightly scribble a soft line on the bottom of your brow with your brow pencil on an angle up toward the second dot at your arch. Now go back and softly scribble a parallel line on the top of your brow as well. Now you should have the beginning of a shape.

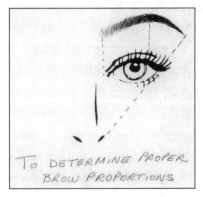

From the arch to the tail of your brow, follow the top of your brow to where the third dot was placed. Now, from the bottom of the arch to the end or tail, meet the top by creating an elongated triangle so that the end of your brow is skinnier than when it starts from the arch.

Fill in using light hair-like strokes, if necessary.

9. HIGHLIGHTER PENCIL

Next, follow your brow application with a highlighter pencil. There are tons of them on the market. Some are frosted; some are not. Some are white; some are pink, gold, or silver. I don't care what color you choose, but it should blend with the eye shadow that you plan to use under your brows. What you want to do here is just scribble a line directly underneath your brow. You don't have to be perfect; it doesn't matter because we're going to blend it. Then take your cotton swab and blend it so that you still see it but it's much softer. The reason you do this, besides the fact that you don't want your eye shadow highlighter to get into your eyebrows, is because you also get a very fine line to help you define your brow, to help separate it. Then I use a little bit of brow gel, and I brush the brows up so that they stay where you put them.

10. EYE SHADOW: #1 on eyelids

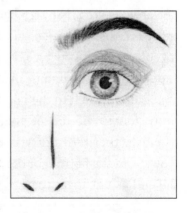

It used to be you had two choices: frosted eye shadow or matte eye shadow. And everybody said, "Oh, when you get older, you have to wear matte because the frost cakes on your lids." Today, the formulas are so different that you don't always have to follow this guideline, because the frost isn't necessarily a frost. It can be more of a sparkle or soft glow than it is a frost. To make a nice simple makeup, you're going to use a matte. So now you take your eye shadow and just blend it onto your upper lid. Go a little bit above the crease, because you want to open up your eyes and make them look bigger.

11. EYE SHADOW—#2 from crease up to brow

Then you're going to select a highlight eye shadow to use from the crease up to the highlighter pencil you have softly blended. You should choose the highlight shadow in a much lighter shade of the color you're using on your lid. Now blend both colors together at the crease line. You shouldn't be able to tell where one ends and the other begins. Just take your brush and blend 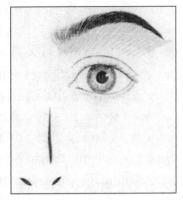 the two together. The kind of brush you want to use is called a lid or eye shadow brush. It's a special brush you use to put on powdered eye shadow.

12. EYELINER

The hard part, for some people, is putting on eyeliner. Some are brilliant at it, but most people struggle with trying to create what they think is a straight line. A lot of people like to use a liquid liner. That's great on young girls, and I think it's fabulous, but as you get older, you 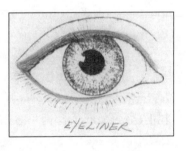 want to have a softer or at least a blendable product to work with. I use a pencil. It's also easier, because if you make a mistake, you can kind of blend it out with some eye shadow. I use brown; then I'll go from brown during the day to black at night. Any soft brown pencil is great, but you do not want to make it too light, because then you're rubbing too hard on your eyelid. What I do is hold and lightly pull from the outside corner of my eyelid so the lid becomes taut and then I can scribble the perfect line. There's no way to make a great line if you try to draw it, so you scribble. That's what I do. I scribble a line across my lid. And I open my eye really big so that I can do the inner corner. There are pencils that come with a smudger so that if you make a mistake, you can just soften the line. Depending on your eye color, you may also choose to use a blue-gray, khaki, or plum pencil instead of brown.

Because my eyes are wide apart, I could, if I wanted, line under my bottom lashes all the way in, but I don't like that "panda" look. What I do is I pull a slight bit on the lower lid to make it taught, and I scribble it, maybe three-quarters of the way in from the outer corner. If you use your lashes as your guide, you can scribble right below the lashes or right into the lashes. If you don't like the way it looks, use your smudger or a dry cotton swab to remove it or to soften the look.

Because I like the softness of a line, what I do is the following: I lift up my top lid a little bit at the corner, and I follow the bottom line and go up to connect to the top line, creating a little V at the corner. Now what I have is big eyes with a slight lift at the ends, à la Sophia Loren or Kim Kardashian.

13. CURL LASHES

To start, you take an eyelash curler and blink to get your lashes into the curler as close to the eyelid as possible. And just hold it. Don't squeeze and undo, squeeze and undo. Just hold. If you get the hang of it, you can walk the curler out to the 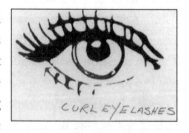 middle and hold again for twenty seconds. Then if you want to get a little bit more of a curl, you can move it out just a little bit and re-curl.

14. MASACARA

I suggest that you put your mascara on before you finish the rest of your eye makeup, in case you mess it up. That way you can clean it up before doing the final eyelid applications.

Take your mascara and start on your upper lid. I use the tip of the brush a lot. I'll brush the lashes out to the side with the tip. Then I'll go back in again and just use the tip to maneuver them around. I try to get all of them, even the ones that are in the inside corner. I like to get as many lashes as I can. Your eyelashes fall out and regenerate all the time, just like your hair. You're always going to have some short ones coming in and some longer ones hanging around.

Now you're going to do the same thing on the bottom. I use the whole brush, but I also use the tip, because the tip helps to move and separate the lashes. Now, you're going to let this eye dry while you do the other eye. When you're dealing with your bottom lashes, you may get flecks of mascara underneath. Don't worry about it. Just wait, let it dry, and then take your dry cotton swab and roll it gently and it'll come off. Don't get freaked out. Nothing's going to happen; you didn't screw up your whole makeup. And it's not because of certain mascaras; it can happen with any of them. Just be careful that you don't buy mascaras that are so wet they just go all over the place. You want a little bit thicker mascara on a brush that has lots of little individual spikes. It makes it clump less. And when you're putting mascara on, move your lashes around with the brush. Move them in toward your nose. Move them back. Then go out to the side. Eventually, you'll get them where they fan. And that's when they look really, really good.

After I've done both eyes, I take the whole mascara brush and hold my eyelashes up for a minute at the base and then kind of walk them out. Then I take the ends with the tip of the brush and fan them out.

You want your lashes to look almost like a fan. Once they're dry, you can, if you want, comb through them with a lash separator, which is like a little comb.

While I'm waiting for all this to dry, I'm not going to do the rest of my eye. I'm going to go down to my face.

15. BLUSH

Blush can be powder, cream, or liquid. Whichever you choose, it should be applied in a kind of C, contoured around the cheekbone and blended upward. Leave at least a finger's width between the bottom of your eye and the top of your cheekbone. If you're using a powder blush, apply it with a nice fluffy powder brush. With cream or liquid, you may use your fingers or a blender sponge. Just know that when you use a sponge, you should be careful not to blend all the color away. The sponge can suck up a lot of the color. I generally put a little color around my hairline or

on my forehead as well as on my chin so that my face has an all-over warmth and it doesn't look like I plopped color just on my cheeks.

16. CONTOUR AND HIGHLIGHTER

Younger women can get away with a lot of contours and highlights. Older women already have some of their own contours and don't want to accentuate that. For them highlights work well. For contours use something that's no more than two shades darker than your own face, because once you start getting any darker than that, it's very hard to blend, and you look like you've drawn it on—and you don't want that, especially in the daylight. You want everything to blend. You might want to get a "blender," a special little sponge that helps blend everything together.

Because I'm older and I want my face to have a glow to it and not look matte, I don't use any powder. I use two different products: a liquid or cream blush and a highlighter, which also comes in powder, cream, or liquid. You may have to poke around to find the one you love the most. I prefer the liquid highlighter and blend it on the very top of my cheekbones.

These highlighters come in many colors, so try to coordinate them with your entire makeup color palette. For example, if you are wearing some rose-colored eye shadows and blush, you might pick a light pink highlighter to accent your cheekbones. If you are wearing browns, khakis, and golds, then a light gold would do the trick. If you are choosing to wear a smoky gray palette, then white or soft silver is perfect. If you're dark complexioned, bronze, copper, and gold work beautifully. What a good highlighter does is give you a moist, dewy look, and it highlights your cheekbones just a little bit.

Take the liquid blush (some of them come with a little sponge attached) and squeeze the liquid onto the sponge. Now apply it to your cheeks by dotting the liquid around the cheekbone and blending upward, leaving a finger's width from the top of the blush to the bottom of the eye. Using whatever highlighter you have chosen, dot the highlighter on top of your cheekbone and blend from your hairline to around to where your blush ends. That's it. No big deal. You blend them together, again, with your fingers. Then wait for a minute, because your skin absorbs a lot of product. You can go back with the blush if you need more. For the evening you definitely need more.

All right, now it's time get back to your eyes.

17. FINISHING YOUR EYES

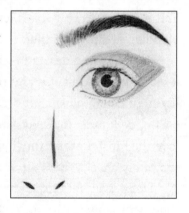

By now the mascara has dried, so I'm going to put on a crease color to contour and give the illusion of opening up the eye. I use my crease brush. It's a rounded brush with a tapered end (they are sold in many beauty stores). I take my color, and where I made the little V on the end where the upper and lower liners meet, that's where I'm going to start. I raise my eyebrows up a little bit, and I start slowly filling in the color. I go over it again and again, working toward the outer corner, because I want it darker at the end and lighter as it goes in toward the nose. I do this, and I just keep blending. Be sure you don't blend it until there's nothing left. If I think I need a little more on one eye, I go back and add a bit more. If you don't have a lot of lashes on the bottom and you want to have that look, take a little bit of that dark shadow and just blend it down under where the eyeliner is and it brings all those colors together.

18. PRIME YOUR LIPS

Let's start with a lip primer, which looks like the concealer for under your eyes, but it's a thinner consistency. You dab it around your lips and JUST blend it in. Then you put your pencil liner on. It makes your liner go on really easily, but it also makes it so that your lipstick doesn't bleed.

19. LIP LINER

Select a lip liner pencil that is close to the lipstick color that you are going to use. Take your lip liner pencil and purse your lips a little bit. I'll tell you why. I don't like the rounded look that's from the 1930s—you know, that kind of

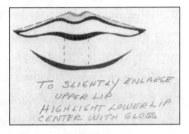

To SLIGHTLY ENLARGE UPPER LIP HIGHLIGHT LOWER LIP CENTER WITH GLOSS

Lucille Ball look. You want your lips to feel like they're going up a little bit at the ends. Purse your lips a little bit and scribble, like you did with the eyeliner pencil—same thing, pencil scribble. Wherever there's a pencil, it's best to scribble to get a perfect line. You can try to draw a straight line, but it's never going to look good. You can scribble it until you get it the way you want. I do one side and then the other side, and then I join them together.

20. LIPSTICK AND GLOSS

Now, using either a lipstick brush or the tube, you fill in your lips with the color you have selected. I like to add a little gloss to the center of the lips for a poutier look.

DONE!

There it is. My makeup is on. I have a lot of makeup on my eyes, so I don't really want to have a bright lipstick during the day. If I wasn't going to put a lot of eye makeup on, then I would want to make sure that I had blush and lipstick, because, otherwise, I'd look like I was dead. You've got to have one or the other.

• • •

DAY TO NIGHT

So now it's nighttime. You're going out, and you want to look more dramatic. Remember that because it's night, the lighting is darker in restaurants, at events, and on the street. You want to pump up the intensity of everything so you won't look washed out.

You're not going to change much. There are only three things that you do differently. You want a color with more pizazz on your eyelids. You would use a gold or something with more iridescence. Then you're going to take your crease brush and use a little bit deeper color in the crease. (It could be dark brown or dark gray or the dark liner you had on during the day.) Take the darker liner, go across your lid, get to the end, make the V, go under the lashes, and work it until you get the look you like. Then go back and give your eyelashes a little more curl and a little brush of mascara again. If you plan to use false eyelashes, this is the time to put them on.

In five minutes, you've made your look go from day to night, and that's all it takes.

This may seem complicated, but I promise you with practice it will become second nature. The rewards will be immeasurable, and, best of all, you'll be proud of the face you're presenting to the world.

SIMPLE STEPS:
REMEMBERING WHAT I"VE TAUGHT YOU

(You might want to make a copy of these instructions and put them on your mirror as a handy reminder until they become second nature.)

1. Cleanse skin thoroughly.

2. Moisturize and let dry.

3. Apply silicone primer and let dry.

4. Blend lightweight foundation, mineral tint, or moisture tint all over face.

5. Dot liquid concealer under eyes and blend with a foundation brush.

6. Using a stick foundation that matches your skin, cover up red areas and dark spots. Apply a little to create a base for your eyelids.

7. Powder is optional. It can be aging, so omit unless you have oily skin.

8. Fill in brows, if necessary.

9. Scribble a white or light highlighter pencil under the brow line and blend with a cotton swab.

10. Apply eye shadow to entire lid from lash to crease with a shadow brush.

11. Using the same shadow brush, blend a lighter highlight shade from your crease to under the brow, right up to the blended white pencil line. Note: The lower lid shadow and the highlight color should blend together seamlessly.

12. Using a pencil or liquid liner, line upper lid first and then apply the liner under your lower lashes.

13. Curl lashes with an eyelash curler.

14. Apply mascara to top lashes first and then to lower lashes.

15. With a blush brush and a soft powder blush, contour a C on both cheeks, then blend. If you choose to use a cream or liquid blush, use fingers or a blender (sponge) to apply and distribute.

16. Using highlighters, contour your face.

17. Using a deeper eye shadow color in the same color tones as your first two shadows, with a crease brush, contour just above the crease, concentrating the darkest area at the outside ends of your eyes. Try to create a soft triangle.

18. Dot a lip primer or a little stick foundation around your lips before applying your lip liner pencil.

19. Line lips with a pencil that is close, color wise, to your lipstick.

20. Apply lipstick with either a lipstick brush or the tube if your lips are full enough, then blend a little gloss in the center of your lips to give you a soft pouty lip.

QUICKIE MAKEUP (Five Minutes)

For those of you who just want to look presentable to go to the market, run errands, or possibly work out (if you feel you need a little makeup), here is the short list:

1. Always start with a clean face.

2. Lightly moisturize.

3. Apply a light tinted moisturizer with an SPF (sun block) of 15 to 20.

4. With a blush brush lightly apply some blush powder color to your cheeks, forehead, and chin. With what is left on your brush, sweep the remaining blush over your entire eyelids.

5. Curl lashes. Mascara is optional.

6. Use a lip gloss in the same color tone as your blush.

7. That's it! You are ready to go. The tint will even out your skin tone, the blush will warm up your complexion, and the gloss will make you look alive. By following these suggestions that take less than five minutes, you will feel confident in how you present yourself to the public.

ACKNOWLEDGMENTS

I began writing this book on my own. One day in my makeup studio, I read an excerpt to a wonderful client who happens to be a literary agent. Her name is Deborah Miller, and she thought I might be onto something. She suggested I meet with Marion Rosenberg, another agent in the literary field and a film producer. We met, I gave her the few chapters I had written, and she was willing to tweak and correct what I had put down so far.

Then things came to a standstill as it became evident that I needed help from a writer who could carry me through the process of writing my book by interviewing me and putting together a manuscript based on a lively exchange between us over many months.

Enter Judy Chaikin, a writer with Write Wisdom. Marion had, with my permission, sent Judy a copy of where we were so far. Judy shared my enthusiasm for the book I hoped to write. It seems that Judy and I had a lot in common. Her husband was a studio musician, as was my father, and we both spent many years in Studio City frequenting a lot of the same places. We hit it off immediately, and Judy's guidance and input were just what I needed to continue.

Three wonderful women who believed in me saw the big picture and helped me through to the end. I cannot express enough how thankful I am to all of them.

Also, to Loren Stephens from Write Wisdom, who agreed to collaborate with Judy and me to make my story *Raising Eyebrows* into an interesting and fun read.

Hugs and thank you to Jenna McCarthy, my little guardian angel on this project.

A special thank you to Ian Dawson for scanning and cleaning up all the vintage photos—eighty plus of them!

And a thank you to the Jenkins Group: Jerry, Andrew, Leah and Yvonne for the final touches on the book you hold in your hand today.

My life is so full of cheerleaders who, with love, curiosity, and determination, pushed me through this process. I was determined to make this book happen, no matter what.

The list is long when it comes to my friends.

Sharon Berchin Hughes, my oldest friend, for being there, whether we talk, see each other, or not. Thanks for all your memories.

Linda Klauss, my "sister" from another mother, and Marty Klauss, for our long and storied history. You guys are truly my memory.

Kim Bryan, another "sister," best listener, creative designer, and most loving friend.

Patti Altbaum Mazzarini, my third "sister," most creative and accomplished woman.

Randy Fuhrman, my brilliant, creative, giving, loving friend. There aren't enough adjectives for you. As Randy was losing his fight with cancer, I was able to read him excerpts from this book and share photos of our fifty years of a wonderful friendship. I already miss you. Rest in peace, my friend.

Sal Abaunza, my "brother" from another mother!

Shelley Stark, my biggest cheerleader.

Lenore King, my "unpaid therapist," voice of reason, and her husband, Michael King, the couple with whom we share so much of our lives.

I love you all. You have helped me realize my potential. Thank you. My friends and family from near and far in no particular order:

Alan and Laura Salter, Bonnie and Offer Nissenbaum, Judie Fenton, Lillian and Stuart Raffel, Vicky Mense, Todd Johnson, Thomas Blumenthal, Ricci Stephenson, Fabiola Ortiz, Harris Shepard, Victoria Thomas, Camille Harichand, Nelson Chan, Richard Huerta, Chris Garcia, Masako Sasaki, Eileen Norton, Travis London, Eugenia Weston, Carole Kopple, Michelle Birke, Stefanie Blase Wine, Jason Pirro, Dave and Janice Saks, Ron and Eva Dworitz, Howard Dawson, Phyllis Smilen, Rabbi Yocheved Mintz, Rabbi David and Adrienne Baron, Mark Rubin, M.D., Robert Huizenga, M.D., John Joseph, M.D., Paul Canter, Allen Edwards and my mahjong group: Beverly Kessler Deborah Green, Nancy Lichtenstein, Mary Presser, Linda Monastirsky, Kim Bryan, and Patti Mazzarini.

A very grateful thank you to Kelly Francis, my former assistant, makeup artist, and right arm. You kept me focused, were my tech genius, and, most of all, my last girl standing.

Hugs to Billy Del Puerto for his creative input and illustrations in the book and for your constant encouragement.

Special thanks also to Bonnie Garvin, who encouraged me to do this book long ago, and, most especially, Orly Garber for her brilliance in coming up with the title of this book.

And Jon Peters and Herb Budoff for believing in such an inexperienced girl.

My loyal clients. Warmest hugs to all of you.

To my dearest Barbara Mandrell, with love and affection to you, to our friendship, to our working relationship, and to our families. It's been a joy traveling this road with you.

To Dolly Parton, who is the smartest, cleverest, and most creative woman I know. Thank you for allowing me into your life.

And to Sean and Mackenzie Astin, whom I've known and loved since they were little, and their father, John Astin, and their wonderful mother, Anna (Patty Duke) Pearce. May she rest in peace.

To my children. My best creations! You have given me many, many reasons to be proud of you both.

I love you, Ian. We grew up together, and I learned slowly how to be a good parent. You are now passing those lessons on to your children. You are a smart, creative, seven-time Emmy award-winning producer, and brilliant photographer, with more to come.

Portia, you are exceeding the best version of what I tried to teach you. You are an incredible parent, a loving wife, a thoughtful daughter, a beautiful homemaker, and an amazing cook, actress, interior designer, and artist.

Carol, my daughter-in-law, a hardworking, smart, loving mother to two fabulous children. Thank you.

Sean, my son-in-law, thank you for being such a devoted husband and dad to my other two fabulous grandchildren.

To my grandchildren, Mia, Pearl, Max, and Levi. I hope this book will, as you get older, give you some understanding of your history. I love you all with all my heart and want all of you to strive to be the absolute best people you can be.

Last, but never least, the love of my life, Mitch. My best friend, lover, caregiver, provider, and comedian. You have selflessly loved and cared for me and our children for much more than half of our lives. Sometimes I think it's what makes you the happiest, and that just makes me love you more, if that's possible. Also, I am overwhelmed with pride for all you have accomplished and how much time and energy you have given to not only city causes but also charitable causes. You are my rock!

My parents

Carol, Ian, Mitch, me, Portia, and Sean

213

Me as a very proud mom with my children, Ian Seth Dawson and Portia Dawson Furst

Portia and me at my milestone seventieth birthday party at the Peninsula Hotel, Beverly Hills

Mitch, almost 43 years married

Mia Rachel Dawson, first born
of Ian and Carol Dawson

Pearl Lou Furst, first born of Portia and Sean Furst

Max Anton Dawson, son of Ian and Carol Dawson

Levi Moses Furst, son of Portia and Sean Furst